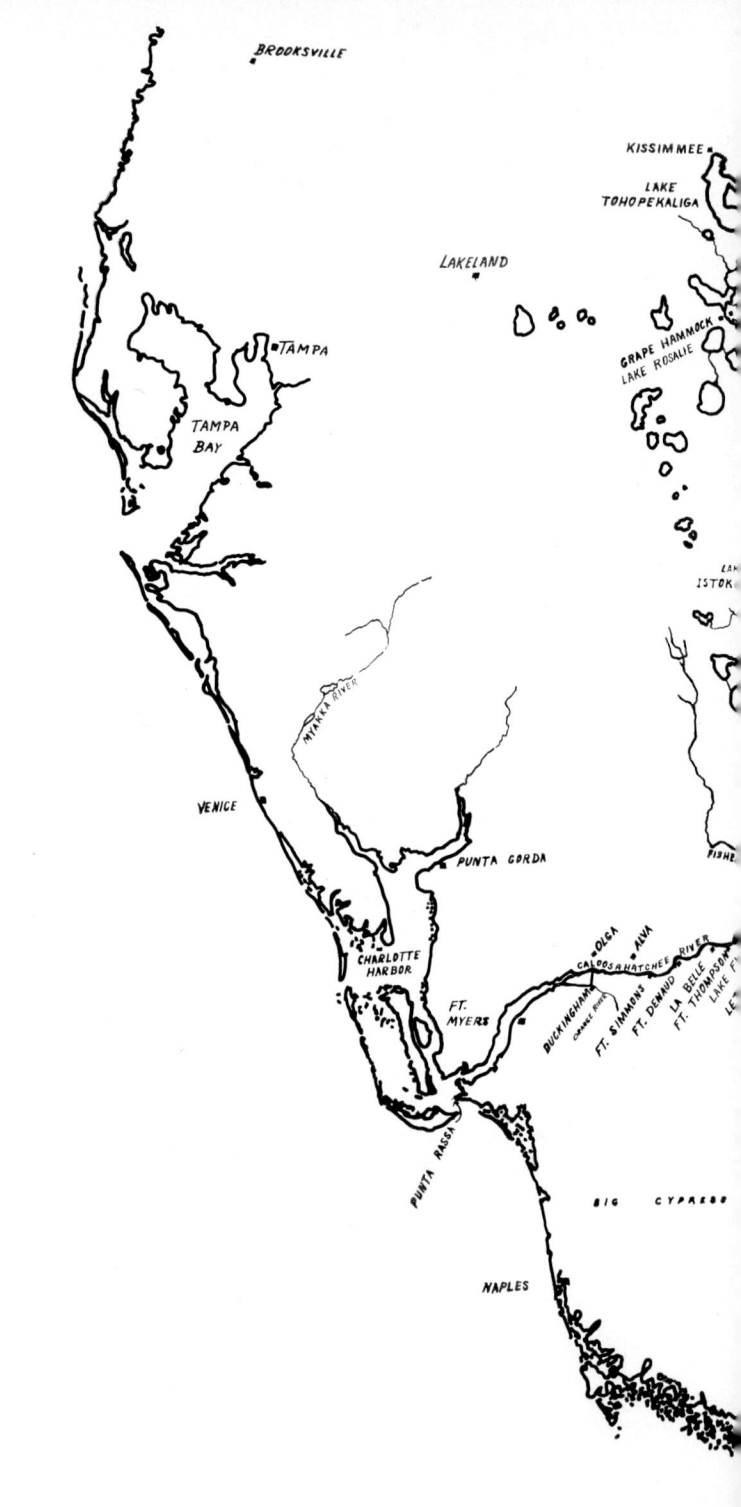

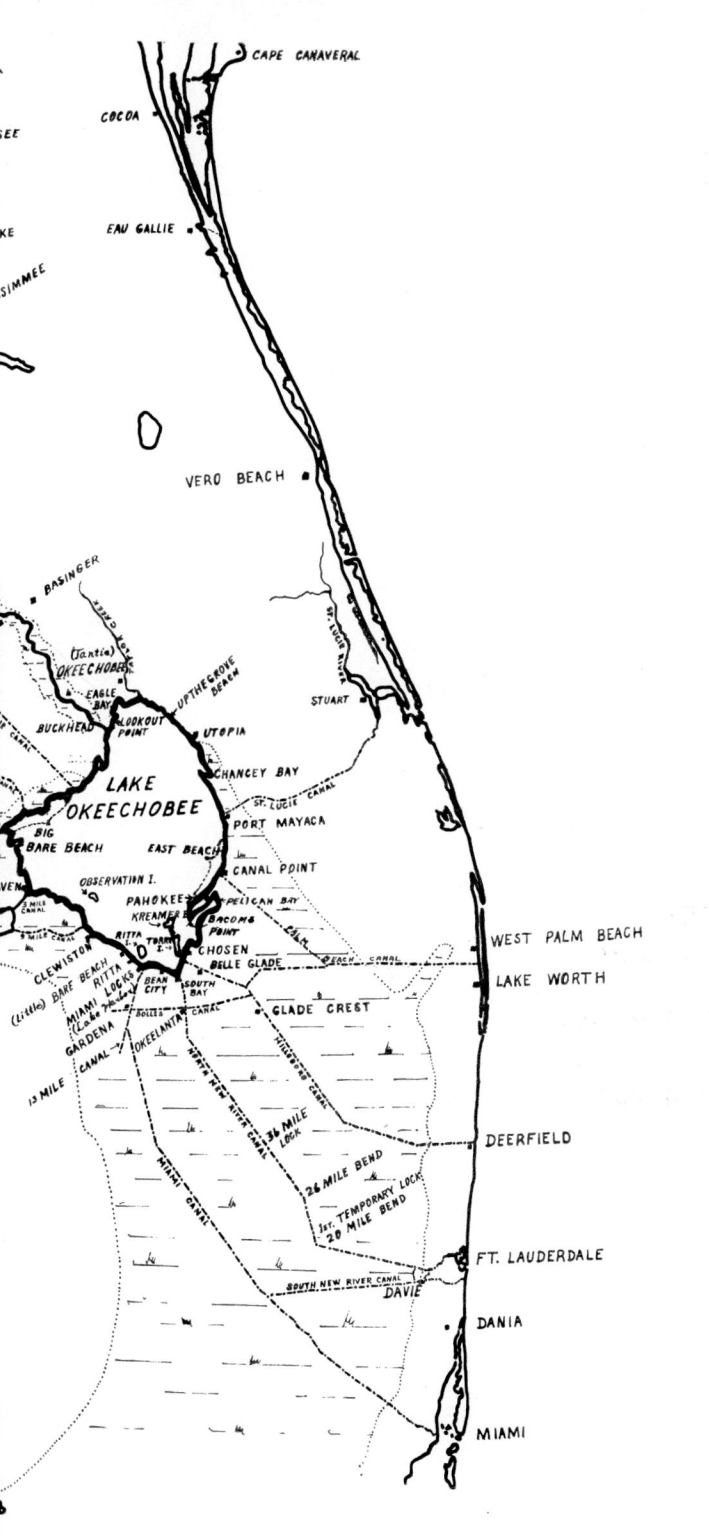

A Pioneer Boatman Tells of

Okeechobee
Boats & Skippers

by

Lawrence E. Will

Cracker Historian and author of

A CRACKER HISTORY OF OKEECHOBEE

— also —

OKEECHOBEE HURICANE
AND THE HOOVER DIKE

GREAT OUTDOORS PUBLISHING CO.
St. Petersburg, Fla.

Meet the *Author*

Lawrence E. Will, "Cracker Historian of the Everglades", writes with authority and understanding of the pioneer days of that region. The author has had an active and a varied part in its development from the beginning of its reclamation until the present.

In 1913, he, with four others, came to the Everglades and started the settlement of Okeelanta, and were the first to try farming in t h e newly drained sawgrass country. Later, as a licensed operator o f passenger and freight boats, he engaged in transportation between settlements on Lake Okeechobee a n d cities of the East Coast,

LAWRENCE ELMER WILL

for it was many years before roads of any kind penetrated to this almost inaccessible region. In addition he operated tow boats and also floating dredges in all parts of the Glades, and during the Boom and Prohibition days he ran a boat yard in Ft. Lauderdale.

In 1927 Will came to his present home, Belle Glade, now largest city of the Everglades, but then a frontier settlement. Here he started a garage, now an auto parts store, which is the oldest business in the city. While serving on the town council he organized a fire department and was for 30 years its chief, meanwhile acting as bus agent for 26 years.

Although still engaged in his store and farming activities, much of his time is now devoted to recording the activities and colorful characters of the early pioneering days when Lake Okeechobee and the Everglades were in their primitive state.

CONTENTS

CHAPTER ONE

Boating Days

Folks talk about the romance of water transportation, well sir, they should have been here on Okeechobee Lake during the boating days. We had more boats here than Carter had liver pills, and we had some skippers who were legends in their own day and time. This lake was the last stomping grounds for steamboats in this state. Those smoke boats once had splashed their way on every watercourse in Florida, always just one jump ahead of civilization. They'd helped to settle up the Kissimmee valley and the Caloosahatchee country as well, but when the water was drained off these Everglades and folks had started to settle here, those wet-tail boats were the first to bring them in, across the lake and down those new dug canals. Then came the gasoline engined boats hauling freight and passengers too, and run boats for to fetch catfish to town, and tugs to tend the floating dredges. Every settler had his skiff boat or launch and the red skinned Seminoles used dugout canoes. We even had store boats and a church boat too. There were no roads and blamed few trails, so if you didn't have a boat you just plain stayed at home. I reckon that we did have some boats on this lake back then, and here's the reason why. This lake was plumb surrounded by the impassible Everglades on its southern half, by swamps and marshes on its other sides. It was only in a few places on its north side that horseback or ox team travel was possible at all.

The first boats for to navigate this lake had been, I reckon, those that the soldiers used during the Seminole War, and that was 130 years ago. Their little sailboats had been built on the river banks or else hauled on ox carts overland. It wasn't till Disston opened the Kissimmee and the Caloosahatchee rivers to his town up state that there was ever ary a steamboat here on Okeechobee Lake, but after that there was a plumb sloosh of them. Stern wheelers they most always were, burning lightered wood. Folks used to call them "wet ass boats" but that don't look too good in print, so I'll just refer to them as "wet tail boats" from here on out. It all means the same thing anyways.

Catfishing was the only business on the big lake in those early days. This lake shore and all that sawgrass Everglades was brand new country then. But when the Everglades land was put on sale, that's when those land hungry, hard hatted Yankee touristers came here to view the "Everglades Promised Land", and every blessed one of them had to come by boat. It wasn't long before settlements began to spring up along the shore and on those Glades canals. For a right long spell of years boats were the only transportation for these settlers and for the tomatoes and beans and peppers which they raised. As farmers and settlements increased in number, so did boats of every kind, and boat business was right smart active until those hurricanes in 1926 and '28 destoyed so many boats and even some of the settlements too. But anyway, before this time we had railroads to the shore and were beginning to get some highways too, so there was no need for boating any more. No need that is, excepting for the catfishing industry which continued for a right smart longer.

Now, what kinds of people lived here when this lake was getting settled up? Those who came to the Everglades sawgrass settlements, and when the Glades were flooded out, drifted to the lake, were mostly from the mid-west states, and a right good share of them had never farmed before. They all were naturally classed as Yankees. The hunters, the cow men on the Kissimmee prairies, the catfishers, and a goodly share of the boatmen too, were native born Florida or Georgia Crackers, a quite different breed of men, I'll have you to know. They could be right at home with only a blanket for a bed and a mosquito bar for a roof, but they weren't really quite so wild as the Seminoles, although those Yankees seemed to think they were, and their Cracker dialect sounded right strange to Northern ears. Now, to be sure, those of them still living would never talk in that way now, but since I'm a-fixing for to take you back to the frontier days and relate some tales of those old boys, don't be surprised if you hear them talking that old lingo now and again.

And the skippers of those old smoke boats, what kind of men were they? Whether they'd come, like Ben F. Hall, from the Ohio River, or from Louisiana, as Clay Johnson and the Menges did, or whether they'd originated right here in Florida, they were a tough and hardy breed, for sure, and brother, they knew all the tricks of shallow water navigation. That they had to know.

But steamboats had to have big crews, which was one reason that the gas powered boats took over. Since the boiler and the engines were at opposite ends of the deck, there must be both a fireman and an engineer, as well as the pilot in the wheel house overhead. On a passenger boat there had to be a cook, for they fed those tourists well, and that's not counting deck hands. A gasoline engine boat. on the other hand, needed only a pilot and an engineer, and he did what little cooking that was done. He didn't even need to be licensed either, though the captain usually was. Those power boat men

I knew right well, for I was one for a right smart while. Hard working men they were, sometimes hard drinking too, whensomever they got to town, but a self reliant, rough and ready lot. To them it was no hardship to sleep with the bare deck for a mattress and an army overcoat for a blanket. If the steering wheel was outside, then brother, they'd get all the benefit of the weather too—rain, hot sun, or worse yet, cold, they'd have to take it all and like it. No eight hour day nor overtime. As one fish boat runner lately said to me,

"A forty hour week? Listen, pardner, I've often worked forty hours between sleeps!" And come to think of it, so have I.

Those power boat men were an unassuming bunch. No skipper was called "captain" unless he had a passenger run, and mighty few even wore a boatman's cap. They didn't want those country folks to think they would put on airs because they ran a boat.

And what about the engines that we had? Well, friend, there's no engine so reliable as steam. The only weak part of a steam rig might be the boiler, and on some of those old wet tail boats it took a plumb good fireman to keep a head of steam. But some of those early gasoline engines we had to depend on would often make you want to cuss, or maybe even, cry! The first were big one or two cylinder heavy duty jobs of the two cycle type. A cylinder would fire each time the piston came up, and the ignition was called "make and break". The firing points were inside the cylinder and the electricity was furnished by five dry batteries and a low tension coil—just some turns of copper wire around an iron core. Water didn't hurt this ignition system, so it was popular for a long time, especially in open launches, but boy, oh boy, how those two cycle engines could give you grief!

Then came the four cycle engines, using valves and spark plugs, timers and high tension coils. These were a heap of improvement, though you had to keep the

engine dry, but even they lacked a heap of being per-
fection. Most of the first of these "four cycles" had only
one cylinder and a mighty heavy flywheel. You'd hear
the exhaust explode with an ear shattering "pow!" You'd
listen till you were positive that the engine had surely
quit. Then she'd bang out another "pow" and keep going
merrily on her way. Later on, of course, we had two, three
and four cylinder engines, and after awhile some sixes,
but I recollect only a couple of Diesels on the lake—a
dredge company's tug and a freighter.

Now, when I said those boatmen were a hardy set,
that's exactly what I meant. They had to be, to wrestle
barrels of flour, drums of gasoline and two hundred
pound sacks of spuds. And if your boat ran hard and
fast aground, you'd have to maneuver some way to get
her a-loose, if'n it took bull strength. And resourceful,
did I say? Suppose your engine conked out in some God
forsaken spot. You'd have to fix it, mister, if'n it taken
blood (from mosquito bites), sweat, cuss words and bal-
ing wire. Every boatman had to be more or less mechanic.
If a pin or key sheared off, you'd hunt around for wire
or nails to fit the hole. If a timer tore plumb up, you
might have to rig one on the propeller shaft, using a
hacksaw blade for a timer brush, as a man I knew did
when stranded on the Kissimmee.

I once had a connecting rod knock out at Fifteen Mile
Post, while running the big NEW RIVER. Did I wait for
somebody to tow me back to Lauderdale? Don't be ridic-
ulous, Mack! In my tool box was some of everything. I
just took out that rod, melted babbit in a frypan over a
canal bank fire, then, by using Octagon soap for a mold,
poured the bearing, scraped it to a fit, and ran on up
to the lake and back. Another time, in NEW OKEE-
LANTA, some teeth on the engine's water pump stripped
off. The gear was brass, so by drilling holes with a carpenter's breast drill, driving nails into the holes, then
dressing them to size, I had a gear which lasted for

several trips. But while all this was being done, the boat
was never stopped. A passenger, with the bilge pump,
kept the cooling water flowing.

The hours were long, the work was hard and right
unpleasant sometimes, yet boating had a fascination all
its own. Standing at the steering wheel or loafing along
side the engine, while listening to the whisper of exhaust-
ing steam and the busy splash of paddles, or to the gas
engine's steady rumble, it sure beat staring a mule in
the tail behind a plow. And to watch the glory of a sun-
rise, a sunset, the stars at night, mossy cypresses on a
river's banks, or the changing face of the lake in glassy
calm, a morning fog, or while rippling before a breeze,
or even the endless unbroken sawgrass of the Everglades,
somehow seemed to inspire you with an admiration of
nature and a feeling of supreme content. You'd never
get that kind of satisfaction while working in a store
or shop. Maybe that's why a sure enough, dyed-in-the-
wool boatman would never stay ashore. So now let's turn
back the calendar a bit to learn about the steamers and
the power boats that those old boys used to run before
highways were built here around the lake.

Those were the days of romance and adventure on
this lake, but those old timey boats are long gone now.
Their skippers have most all passed away. So before it's
all forgot, it wouldn't do no harm to tell what those boating days were like, and sort of get acquainted with their
skippers too—J. Fred and "Connie" Menge, Ben Franklin Hall and Ed Hall too, Ad Gilbert, Clay Johnson and
all the Murrays. And the power boat men like Felix
Forbes, that famous rum runner Bill McCoy, John Ziegler, John Aunapu and Big Foot Bill. Heck, I used to
know most all of them and some were most bodacious
characters, I'm telling you for sure. Some other time I'll
try to get around to telling about the catfish seining
boys, and how they loved to fight and frolic, but now
let's hear about those "wet tail boats".

CHAPTER TWO

Cruise of the BERTHA LEE

So you're a-fixing to take your outboard motor boat and j'ine in that there Boat-A-Cade from Kissimmee down the river to Okeechobee Lake? Well son, if'n I weren't so doggone old and half stove up I'll be dadburned if I wouldn't love to go along myself. I'd give a purty just to see that old river again, jist to see how much hit's changed since the old steamboatin' days. Oh, I know the river's changed, everything else has changed in fifty years, but I know blamed good and well hit hasn't changed like these Everglades and Lake Okeechobee has done. When I first come to this lake, my boy, you'd scarce believe it now, but where all the towns and cities are, there wasn't a crying soul a-livin' here on this lake shore excusin' only a few catfishermen in their tarpaper shacks and some folks at a land company's hotel at Ritta —what we call Lake Harbor now. Only them and a scattering of hunters killing off the alligators and the last of the egrets for their feathers—they was worth their weight in gold, them plumes was then.

After the settlers begun to driftin' in I used to freight their vegetables from Pahokee, Little Bare Beach and Ritta down the canal to Ft. Lauderdale, a pow'ful long and monotonous haul. From the custard apple woods along the lake shore, spang down to Ft. Lauderdale—sixty one miles hit were—you'd see nothin' from the pilot house excusin' only sawgrass as far around as you could look. Just sawgrass all that day-long trip, a-wavin' and a-glistening in the sun, head high to a tall Seminole, a-growin' thar in that shallow water of the Glades. And now hit's all in cattle pastures and vegetables and sugar cane.

Hit were when I was a-boatin' on the big lake that I got to know some of them old Kissimmee River steamboats and their crews and especially Cap'n Clay Johnson, the most famous one of all. He were the last man to run a steamboat in the State of Fluridy. But before I git to tellin' you of him, I'd jist as well to tell you something about the Kissimmee River itself, and all the old timey smoke boats that used to run on hit.

That Kissimmee River now—if'n you want to hear about steamboatin' on that river, son, you'd just as well go back to the beginning of hit, and that of course, was Disston. When Hamilton Disston, the moneyed sawmaker, bought four million acres of South Fluridy back in 1881, that made him the owner of a huge scope of territory, from Orlando clear down to 25 miles south of Lake Okeechobee, but Disston made his headquarters in Kissimmee at the railroad's end. There'd never been but one steamboat at Kissimmee up till then, but Disston needed steamers for his work and the settlers that he brought in needed them to haul their oranges and gator hides, and then was when the Kissimmee began to swarm with steamboats churning the river into foam and spoutin' clouds of lightered smoke.

Hit were in the little trading post of Kissimmee that Disston built his shops and foundries and boat yards on the shore of Lake Tohopekaliga, right spang where the city park and zoo now lays, and Kissimmee become a boat building town. First off Disston built hisself some

dredges, for he aimed to drain his land and to open up a
waterway from his town in the center of the state clear
to the Gulf of Mexico. He connected Lake Tohopekaliga
with Cypress Lake and Lake Hatchinaha and Lake Kissimmee to the Kissimmee River which empties into Lake
Okeechobee. And then, by Neds, he hired the Menge
brothers from Louisiana to clear the snags and logs from
the Caloosahatchee, dredge out the falls at Ft. Thompson
and dig a canal from Lake Flirt up to Lake Okeechobee
from the other direction, and so he had his waterway
from Kissimmee to Ft. Myers, the same one you aim to
travel on your Boat-A-Cade.

And then of course, he had to have some boats to
tend his dredges. In 1882 they launched the OKEECHO-

Steamer OKEECHOBEE built by Capt. R. E. Rose for the Disston
Land Co. Used as dredge tender and for inspection trips by officials.
Here she is shown in Lake Cypress loaded with cord wood for the
dredge cutting the Hart Canal to St. Johns River. This canal, however, was never completed.

BEE and a couple of years later the 41 foot ROSALIE, steamboats with cabins for the workmen. And I reckon that you might be surprised to know that one of his boats had for a passenger the president of these Newnited States. This was the 64 foot HAMILTON DISSTON, built in Philadelphia back in 1872. After the canals had been dredged out deep enough for her 6.8 foot draft, she was brought to Ft. Myers and then up the Kissimmee, and at Southport they held a ceremony for to honor president Chester A. Arthur. Now, the president was used to ceremonies, to be shore, but when he caught a ten pound bass he allowed as how there was no place like this, even though hit were plumb outside the edge of civilization.

And John Jacob Astor taken a honeymoon trip down the river on one of Disston's boats, slap down to Lake

The Original HAMILTON DISSTON, Capt. Mike Grogan. Her Cabin and Upper Works overhung her hull. She was so top heavy that she nearly sunk twice, so was finally used as a warehouse at Kissimmee.

Okeechobee and back. Then Thomas A. Edison decided to cruise down the Kissimmee to his winter home in Ft. Myers, but he must have left his rabbit's foot at home. His boat, a second one named HAMILTON DISSTON, got hard and fast aground in the shallows near South-port, so, disgusted with such a sorry start, he hailed the upbound TALLULAH and departed from Kissimmee on the train.

But now, son, let me tell you about the first big boat ever to steam up to Kissimmee, and a most bodacious cruise that were, I'll have you to know. This here boat were the BERTHA LEE, 130 feet in length and only four years old, and Ed Douglas was her owner. Hit was during the summer of 1883 that she come sailing down the Mississippi from Peoria, Illinois with a load of grain for New Orleans. There Douglas hired for a skipper Cap'n Benjamin Franklin Hall, Jr., and an old time steamboat man he was for shore. At the age of twelve he'd started out as oiler on an Ohio River boat, then he was a cub pilot ontil he was nineteen. That was when he passed his exam and was made captain of the towboat CHARLIE BROWN. The Ohio and the Mississippi was his stomping grounds, but he was hauling steel rails into Pensacola for the L. & N. whensomever the BERTHA LEE arrived.

Steamboating was all that Cap'n Hall knowed, and he was much of a man, for sure. I've heard tell as how he could pick up a 200 pound barrel of flour by hits chimes and heave hit from the deck right onto the gunnel, or trot up the gangplank with a 50 pound sack under each arm. And cuss? He could cuss ontil the oak leaves shrivelled on the trees.

Cap'n Hall fotched the BERTHA LEE from New Orleans to Ft. Myers, and there he met up with Cap'n Lawrence Jennings who'd jist arrived in a little sailboat from Kissimmee, for to meet him and to pilot the boat upriver. Now, this Cap'n Jennings weren't no fool. He knowed his Fluridy rivers, so when Cap'n Hall axed him for to take over and pilot for him, Cap'n Jennings, he studied over the BERTHA LEE'S 130 foot of length and her 3.8 foot of draft, and allowed as how he'd druther not, yit still, he said, he'd go along, for to give what advice he could. Shucks, he wanted to git back home anyways, I reckon.

Loading Cotton On The River

BERTHA LEE at Columbus, Georgia, loading cotton, rosin and turpintine for Apalachicola. She sunk in Moccasin Bend near Bristol, Georgia, a total loss.

'Twas on September the 20th, 1883 that the BERTHA LEE cast off, sailin' grandly up the narrow Caloosahatchee, backin' up and steamin' ahead around them hairpin bends and sendin' a rope ashore to a cabbage tree to get around the worst ones. By the end of the second day she had only got to Ft. Thompson, and then Lake Flirt, a "shallow mudhole" slowed her down some more. Bonnet Lake and Reedy Canal weren't no improvement

I don't reckon, and Lake Hicpochee was worse, but in Three Mile Canal she really stopped. Her guards got hung on the banks and there she stuck ontil a dam was built to float her off. By the end of a week she'd reached the old Flat Top Cypress at the edge of Lake Okeechobee —that's where Moore Haven is now, you know. She didn't have but three cords of lightered wood on board, and so she laid up at Observation Island, whilst the crew cut wood. Then she steamed across Lake Okeechobee to the Kissimmee River, and I reckon that was a new kind of stream to Cap'n Hall.

Captain Benjamin Franklin Hall, Jr., Master, and later owner of the BERTHA LEE.

As fur as he could see thar weren't nothing but wet prairie with here and yonder in the fur distance, a trifling hammock, a cypress head or a clump of cabage trees. Strange lookin' water plants crowded along each river

bank, whilest ducks and cranes and pond birds by the
hundreds, stalked and swum and flew off in plumb clouds
as the boat approached. And Cap'n Hall knowed then
why Cap'n Jennings had refused the piloting job. With
all them by-channels, cutoffs and dead rivers a-ziggin
and a-zagging among the water bonnets and flags and
reeds, with a narrow channel crookeder than ary snake,
and with a current so sluggish that you couldn't tell
which the main channel was, this river was the beatenest
that Cap'n Hall had ever seed. Then further up hit narrowed some, but thar was some of the most bodacious
long bends where you could steam ahead an hour or two
to gain 100 yards. Thar was one place, I'm telling you
for a fact, about as fur acrost as from hyar to that pine
tree yonder, twenty or thirty yards, no more, down Micco
Bluff way hit were, where a boat could steam ahead for
two cussed hours or more to git from one side of that
there neck of land to the other. Hit were old Clay Johnson who fixed that bend. He waited ontil the river was
high, then backed his LILLIE up and fanned a channel
slap acrost that neck with his paddle wheel, and the
river did the rest.

But when I say crooked, I reckon that old river was
some crooked! Thar was one old settler, I don't reckon
he stretched the truth too much, who used to say as how
you could look up some mornin' and see a steamboat's
smoke off to the south'ard, then atter a bit hit'd be to
the east of you, then in the afternoon, when you'd about
forgot to look again, hit would be over towards the settin'
sun. You could onhitch and feed your mule atter you'd
heered her whistle toot, and then go down to the landin'
and watch her splashing by.

Yes siree, this was a new kind of a river to Cap'n
Hall, and he begun to wish that he was back on the good
old Mississippi. He kept his deckhands busy shovellin'
off them bends and pulling cattails off'n his paddle

wheel, but atter a few weeks of this soup-doodle navigation their stock of victuals, like their patience, was a-run-
nin' low, so Cap'n Hall sont a couple of men in a rowboat
to go ahead and fotch some rations back. Hit were a full
week before they returned. They wasn't sca'cely a meal's
victuals left aboard the BERTHA LEE and I reckon the
whole blamed crew might have starved right thar, smack
in the middle of nowhere, if'n some Injuns hadn't happened by who sold them some turkeys for two bits apiece.
The old BERTHA LEE reached Kissimmee, but hit takened her 52 crying days, danged near two months to
make that trip. I reckon Cap'n Hall learned right smart
about Fluridy rivers on that run.

Well, the BERTHA LEE messed around that winter,
makin' a few excursion trips for moneyed tourists, but
when the next summer's rains had put the river at hits'
highest stage, the old boat shook the mud of the Kissimmee from off'n her paddle wheel, and wallered her
way back to the Gulf. But whensomever they got back to
civilization, bless Pete, the crew started to squall for
their back pay. But pore Ed Douglas by that time was
broke as any convict, and he'd jist got hisself married
besides. And so the boat was sold, and Ben Franklin Hall,
who had the biggest claim, he bought her in. Atter that
he run her on the Suwannee River and then on the Ap-
palachicola where she hauled cotton from Columbus,
Georgy, but a year later she up and killed herself on
a snag in the Chattahoochee, and Cap'n Hall come back
to Kissimmee.

His first boat here were the 35 foot side wheeler
SCHIPMAN which some sportsmen had done shipped to
Kissimmee. River business was a-gitting good, so he
bought the 45 foot COLONIST which had been built there
for the Narcoossee Colony, and Cap'n Hall wore her plumb
out in the river trade. In 1892 he built and run the little
30 foot NAOMA I, and five years later the NAOMA II.
With his boat he foched catfish, yes, catfish and egret

feathers too, from his fish camps on Okeechobee Lake, near about the first catfish camps there was on this big lake too, though later on catfishing was a million dollar business. He built and run the CORONA also, but the last boat he owned was the NAOMA III, a 55.4 footer which he'd built in 1901. This is the boat which taken Governor Broward and his cabinet on a couple of their

NAOMA II hauling material for Tampa's first power house above Sulphur Springs. After this contract NAOMA II was brought to Kissimmee, changed to a stern wheeler, and hauled the first catfish from Lake Okeechobee.

inspections of the lake and the canals, and she was chartered to the Smithsonian for to take hits scientists on their exploration trips, a-hunting for old Injun mounds and such. Cap'n Hall was give up to be one of the best pilots on the rivers, and he owned a heap of boats, but he didn't want no more BERTHA LEES.

CHAPTER THREE

Kissimmee River's Wet Tail Boats

For nigh onto forty years steamboating was a right thrivin' business on the old Kissimmee as land hongry settlers and ramblin' hunters begun to populate the valley. Before the railroad had been built into Kissimmee— in 1883 that were—what few settlers and cowmen as

"Wood Up"

A $4.00 cord of Lightered Wood was good for a Day and a Half of Steaming, but to Conserve Cargo Space, only a Half or a Quarter Of a Cord might be taken on at one of the Various Wood Landings along the River.

there was then, rangin' down as fur as to the Caloosahatchee, had used to drive their ox wagons, takin' the
whole blamed family along, all the way to Mellonville
(that's Sanford now), to do their little tradin'. They
might have to travel 100 mile or more and be gone a
couple of weeks. But steam boats put an end to that, and
they brought in a heap of new settlers besides.

But these steamboats was no BERTHA LEES. Lord
no! They was no BERTHA LEES! They was made to
order for this river trade, little and shallow draft and
burning fat pitchy pine for fuel—we'uns called hit lightered wood. Most of them was built in Kissimmee, and
danged near every steamer was a stern wheeler, too. We
used to call 'em "wet tail boats," ha! a right appropriate
name for 'em that was, but them wet tailed boats helped
to settle up the Kissimmee valley. Most all of them run
down to Ft. Bassenger, the furthest settle-ment, a plumb
two day's trip.

Now before Disston had come here and started to do
about, like I was a-sayin', there wasn't but only one steamboat runnin' out of Kissimmee, and hit couldn't git down
to the Kissimmee river ontil them canals was dug. This
boat was the MARY BELLE, and she was owned by Kissimmee's first storekeeper Major Allen, and she was run
by Tom Bass, Sr. That was when Kissimmee was knowed
as Allendale. Later on she was owned by Cap'n Frank
King, till he was blinded and like to have got killed when
a boiler blowed up on him. He got a job as bridge
tender in Tampa after that. Her next skipper was Cap'n
Paul Gibson, whose daughter, Alma Hetherington, has
writ down a heap about those old river boats. MARY
BELLE'S last owner was Cap'n John Pearce, and now I'm
a-fixin' to tell you how that old boat died.

Cap'n Pearce was a-steamin' down to Bassenger with
only a couple of country boys for a crew, but he had to
stop at Grape Hammock for to deliver some goods to

Captain Paul Gibson, one of the early skippers on the Kissimmee.

Willingham. Now this Willingham was a bad actor, to be sure. Everybody was a-scared of him on account of his killin's and his cuttin' up, though I've heard tell he got to be a right decent citizen atter he finally served a term in Raiford. Well, when the MARY BELLE pulled up to the landing, thar was Willingham, drunk as usual and quarrelsome as always. He pulled his knife on Cap'n Pearce, but him and his boys outmanned him and tied him up. Pearce told his boys to take the boat on down to Ft. Bassenger whilst he borrowed an oxcart to take Willingham to the sheriff in Orlando. But the boys got to studyin' that if they was to go thar, when they come back, why, there'd be Willingham a-waitin' for them with a gun. So figurin' out a way to make hit look accidental, they sunk the boat at Ft. Bassenger, and that were the end of the old MARY BELLE.

The MARY BELLE were the first steamboat to run the Kissimmee River and the last one were Cap'n George Steffee's ROSEADA, till that hurricane wrecked her in 1928. But between the days when the MARY BELLE was launched and when the ROSEADA got wrecked, there was such a fleet of little wet tail steamers on this river till you's scarce believe it if'n I was to name 'em all. Back in the 1880's and 1890's thar was the 83 foot MARY DISSTON, brought here from Philadelph-

MARY DISSTON. After the end of Disston's operations this boat was run on Manatee River and at Cedar Keys.

ia. Thar was the 45 foot side wheeler SPRAY built in 1882 and owned by Arch Bass and by Cap'n W. J. Brack who'd been first mayor in Orlando, and thar was the 60 foot SADIE OF SALEM from Massachusetts which later was a tug in Tampa harbor and was rechristened CLARK. Then thar was the 35 footer ARBUCKLE, and the big 105 foot FLORIDELPHIA belonging to the land company of that name, but she went to South America and from there to Los Angeles. One boat, the CINCINNATI, was

The CINCINNATI after Captain Johnson had bought her and named her ROSE ADA. Later, with a new hull, she was christened ROSEADA.

shipped plumb from Chicago on the train in 1889. She belonged to the Ritter Lumber Company on Lake Rosalie till Captain Johnson bought her and named her ROSE ADA. Then in 1893 he gave her a new hull and he renamed his boat ROSEADA. And, of course, thar was the NARCOOSSEE, owned by Missouri Bass, and Tom Bass were her skipper, but she didn't run here very long, and thar was Sol Aultman's LITTLE TAMPA, too.

Cap'n Johnson's big OSCEOLA was being run by his son-in-law, Lon Dann, until that young buck decided as how he wanted to be a boat owner hisself. He built the open power boat ROSEADELE, which was skippered by Cap'n Ed Hall. A land company chartered the boat for to bring prospects down the river to Micco Bluff, where they were put into autos for to view them swamps and palmetto prairies. Most any kind of land looked good those pink eared Yankees.

Thar was the 33 foot TALLULAH built by the Gilbert brothers in 1890 and named for their sister. Atter she sunk in Lake Kissimmee she was raised and rebuilt in 1901 by J. C. Stratford who renamed her REINDEER. Now, that Cap'n Stratford was a man who loved his boat. He was a remittance man from England who had an island in Lake Tohopekaliga, but the crazy knocker was so anxious to git a steamboat master's license that he even give up his English citizenship, and with it his $1700 a year annuity, and so he died pore, but I reckon happy. He had a temper too. They used to tell of how he got so riled at his triflin' son Bert, that he once pushed the boy overboard into the lake and left him to swim ashore as best he could.

Then thar was the 33 footer J. M. KREAMER, built in 1894 and named for Disston's chief engineer, and the OCTAVIA, a 55 footer built in 1891 for the Brown Brothers but she finished up on the Suwannee River. And besides all these thar were W. A. Roebuck's little RUTHIE and his EDNA and his CITY OF BASSENGER too. This boat had been a sailing sharpie, but Cal Buckles had got her, put in a kerosene burning engine and a propeller, and named her IRENE. Then Roebuck bought her for to haul supplies to his store in Bassenger. He put in the boiler, engines and paddle wheel from the NAOMA II and called her CITY OF BASSENGER. Besides all these boats, there was the onlucky JUANITA, and that's still not counting the fleets of the Gilbert Brothers, nor Clay Johnson, neither. Yes, I reckon there actually was some steamboats on this river!

Now, that JUANITA, let me tell you what happened to the old JUANITA. She'd been built by the Mobley brothers, Marion and Walter in 1905. Only 46 foot by 10 she was, a heap too small to be much use, and her

Captain W. A. Roebuck in the wheel house of the
CITY OF BASSENGER.

4" by 16" engines couldn't push her no more than six
miles an hour with 120 pounds of steam. On this trip
that I'm fixing for to tell you about, she'd come down
from Kissimmee with a full load of merchandise, including for one thing, fifteen barrels of flour, and she was
loaded to her guards. They'd crossed Lake Kissimmee
and tied up at Turkey Hammock where they takened on
a right good jag of cypress shingles piled high on her
decks for to finish up the load. Hit was atter dark
whensomever they pulled away, but unbeknownst to the
crew, whilst they'd been a-loading her, all the top seams
in her hull, dried out and open, had been gulping down
water till her bilges were right well filled. Well, the old
boat pulled away from the dock, and as her skipper rolled
his wheel like mad to get her straightened out in the
river channel, bless goodness, half that deck load of

LUCY B. owned by Cal Buckles. The last steamboat built in Kissimmee.

cypress shingles went overboard on one side, whilst the
top heavy boat rolled over the other way and capsized.
Only part of one gunnel showed above the river. Nobody
got hurt, thank the Lord, and in the next few days they
dived around and got up most of the cargo, including
that fifteen barrels of flour. The water hadn't penetrated
far so some of the flour was saved, but the barrels busted
open and the range cows ate that sour dough and a
whole slush of them up and died, but worse yet, the
Mobleys had to pay for that lost merchanise, and so
they went plumb broke. A man named Jordan bought
the boat for to carry fish, but by Neds, Jordan he went
broke too. So then Jim Prevatt and Paul Gibson and Harmon Raulerson tried her for a while, but they passed her
on to the Minnix brothers, who sold her hull to Cap'n
Johnson for a barge and Cal Buckles got her machinery.
Cal had just built the LUCY B, a 50 foot boat that he
was a-fixing to use in building a sea wall at Kissimmee.

CITY OF ATHENS. Left to right—James R. Gilbert, Captain, Herb Fleming, Sr. and Herb Fleming, Jr. (Sponsors), H. S. Gilbert (kneeling), Edward Gilbert, Enoch Albritton, Sam Gilbert, Jack Hancock. Standing on steps is Sam's wife Polly while holding to the stanchion is Ad's wife Ellen.

Buckles used her for a house boat atter steamboating went sour. It were in 1912 that the LUCY B was built and she were the last steamboat ever to be built in Kissimmee, and at Kissimmee the LUCY B ended her days.

But the really big operators on the Kissimmee was those Gilbert brothers. Five of them, there was, but the only one I knowed were Addison S., Cap'n Ad we always called him. Now son, I know you aint a-thinkin' yit about bein' old, but you needn't to dread it ere a bit if'n you can git old like Cap'n Ad. When last I seed old Cap'n Ad, in 1959 hit were, he'd just turned 91 years of age, but with his silvery hair, and his starched white shirt and tie, he was a plumb sight to see, and his mind, son, hit were just as chipper as a kildee on a frosty mornin'. Talkin' to a man who'd been a steamboat skipper back in Disston's day, when Injuns and cowhunters was thicker in these woods than insurance agents are now, was like turnin' back the pages of a history book.

ROSALIE, Captain R. E. Rose, in Lake Flirt. She finally sunk near
here in the Ft. Thompson rapids.

Cap'n Ad had come to Kissimmee from Leesburg,
Georgia in 1886 and about the first thing he did was to
make a trip to Lake Okeechobee. The dredge HAMIL-
TON DISSTON had jist finished diggin' the Thirteen
Mile Canal at Ritta thar, and Ad Gilbert joined the crew
of the ROSALIE when she steamed down to the big lake
to dismantle the machinery and tow the dredge back up
to Kissimmee. Cap'n Ad says it took two hard weeks of
work to take that machinery down and load it onto a
couple of barges. Then on the night that the ROSALIE
started back, a most bodacious squall overtakened them
jist as they had cleared Ritta Island. The anchors
wouldn't hold and them barges was about to beat the
poor ROSALIE to death and so they cut 'em a-loose.

Atter layin' for three days in the island's lee, they finally found the barges, but all of the machinery had been lost overboard. The dredge hull they towed acrost the lake and left her in the Kissimmee's mouth, and so far as Ad Gilbert was concerned, she could be a-layin' thar till yet. Well, it weren't too long atter this that them five Gilbert brothers got into the steamboat business for their selves. They not only ran the river, but often times they'd make charter trips slam down to the big lake hitself, and even down on the Caloosahatchee, too. Their first boat, said Cap'n Ad, had been the 65 foot sternwheeler CITY OF ATHENS. She burned and sunk in the Caloosahatchee in 1890, but was bought and rebuilt by the Menge brothers thar. Them Menges, J. Fred and Conrad, was the king bees of the Caloosahatchee River trade. They owned the SUWANEE, the EDISON, the UNEEDA and a heap of other steamers.

But the Gilberts didn't lack for boats. Thar was the TALLULAH till they sold her to Stratford who changed

Sam Gilbert's POLLY. "A sidewheeler and plumb slow one at that."

her name to REINDEER, and the little POLLY, named
for Cap'n Sam's wife. Her machinery was out of Johnson's MAMIE LOWNE. She was a sidewheeler, and a
plumb slow one at that, but she hauled oranges on Lake
Tohopekaliga ontil they sold her hull to Cap'n Bass, and
she ended up her days on the beach at Lookout P'int at
the Kissimmee's mouth.

The Gilbert's last steamer, and their finest one, were
the BASSENGER. The Steamboat Service records says as
how she were built in 1899, but Cap'n Ad said 'twas in
'91. Now, he could be wrong, but not his wife, for she
says she comed to Kissimmee in '91 whilst the BASSEN-
GER were a-building. She knows that date right well, for

BASSENGER at her launching at Kissimmee. High water from a
storm put her afloat prematurely before her "hog chains" had been
installed. Weight of the boiler forward and the engines and paddle
wheel aft, gave her a permanent "hog back".

that's the year she married Ad. This BASSENGER, she were a good sized boat, 67 foot by 17, with six staterooms on her upper deck. The Gilberts finally sold her to B. F. Dewey at Punta Gorda, who put her to towing barges of phosphate to ships in Charlotte Harbor, and Cap'n Tom A. Bass, he were her master then ontil she burned in 1902.

But on the Kissimmee River run Cap'n Ad Gilbert were her skipper and he put out to get the passenger business. The BASSENGER, she was a fast boat too, twelve mile an hour, and that was going some! So, with her fine staterooms for their accommodation, she didn't never lack for passengers, and I reckon that them Gilbert brothers might have had the Bassenger run sewed up, if'n hit hadn't a-been for Cap'n Clay Johnson.

Now thar was a man, my boy, that I just wish you could have knowed!

CHAPTER FOUR

The Last Steamboat Skipper

Maybe you've seed a sternwheel boat a-splashing up some river, pushing a passel of barges along a nice dredged-out channel, with a finger-piling at every bend and a beacon on every sandbar. You seed a guy up thar in the pilot house, and you thought you was a-looking at a steamboat captain. Well son, you aint seed nothing but a floating truck driver, for the last steamboat captain has done tied up in his home port and pulled his fires for the final time. And you won't see ne'er another one, boy, for there's never going to be no more!

Steamboats is finished, son, killed by the railroads and the highways and the diesel engines, yes, and by the high cost of hired help and lightered wood. They was run off from the St. Johns and the Oclawaha, from the Suwannee and the Indian River, then from the Kissimmee and Caloosahatchee, and they made their last stand right hyar on Lake Okeechobee, whilst I were a-boatin' thar.

Now, if you're of a mind to picture the captain of one of them old smoke boats, you'd most likely imagine him standing by his steering wheel, spare and straight, with a big white moustache acrost his lean, tanned face, with keen blue eyes, and a shock of snowy hair crowned by

30

a battered boatman's cap. And so, I reckon you'd have a pretty accurate portrait of old Cap'n Clay Johnson, the last of Fluridy's steamboat skippers. And if'n you'd have told him he was the dead spit of old Mark Twain, he'd a-been your friend for life.

Clay Johnson steamboated whar thar wasn't neither buoys nor beacons nor dredgedout channels, and he had no searchlight to pick up his marks at night, nor ship-to-shore telephone to let his missus know he'd be an hour

Captain Clay Johnson with a grandchild. "Iff'n you'd a-told him that he was the dead spit of old Mark Twain, he'd have been your friend for life."

late in gettin' home, but he could read the face of the water like a parson readin' scripture. He'd never mistake a wind ripple for a sandbar, and he knowed the silver streak that marks a hidden snag, or the lines and curves above a shoal. Likewise, he knowed how the river changes shape in fog or mist or pitchy darkness. Under a slow bell he might nose his boat up some twisting, hyacinth clogged creek that he'd never seed before in his borned life, in water knee deep to a pond bird, and with Spanish moss draped from her funnel stays and cypress branches framming her stern at every bend, knowing blame well that when he delivered his load he couldn't never turn around and would have to back her out for a half a dozen miles or so. Or when the summer rains had swelled the Kissimmee to a mile wide lake, he knowed which of the many channels would git him home the quickest without ramming a stob slam through her bottom. In the narrow, twisty Caloosahatchee he knowed the trick of getting her around them freshet-swelled bends when the current tried to throw her crossways as she poked her nose around the corner. And he could read the clouds and the sky at sunset.

For a heap of years Cap'n Johnson made that river run from Kissimmee acrost Lake Tohopekaliga (folks mostly called hit Lake Toe-hope) through the canal to Cypress Lake and Lake Hatchineha and then down the Kissimmee River, stoppin' at all them river landings, Turkey and Grape Hammocks and Bay Hammock, too, and then you'd come to Kicco, Shell Hammock and Ft. Kissimmee which Colonel Taylor started whilst on his way to fight the Injuns down on Lake Okeechobee. Then he'd stop at Alligator Bluff and Micco Bluff and then Ft. Bassenger. Down below here was Woodyard where he'd take on a cord or so of lightered for his trip back home. There wasn't much at Ft. Bassenger, only jist a couple of stores and the steamboat docks. The main settlement was Bassenger itself, on high ground back from the river a piece. Here thar used to be three stores, big ones too, for that time and place, and two church houses as well. Thar was orange groves and cattle and a right smart of people scattered through them piney woods. Huntin' was big business then and the steamboats brought back skins of otters, coons and gators too, as well as oranges, from every river landing, and sometimes they would git guavas from the Seminoles in exchange for *wyomee* or shine.

For forty years Bassenger were the main town in the lower valley, that is, hit were till a railroad was built to Okeechobee, or Tantie, as we called it then, and that, son, ended steamboatin' on the river. Thar's still some orange groves and cows at Bassenger and one church house, too, but the only store thar now is in a piddlin' fillin' station. Bassenger has done moved to Okeechobee and the steamboats moved thar, too.

I rec'llect one time when Otis Hardin, the civil engineer, had built hisself a big digging machine at Okeechobee, loaded it crosswise on two barges and got Cap'n

Captain Clay Johnson's First Steamer MAMIE LOWNE. Captain Johnson and his Wife in Stern. Their two daughters and "Little Clay" (seated) forward.
The sailboat belonged to Smith Dorien, a florist who propagated roses.

Clay Johnson in his OSCEOLA and me in the gasoline powered tug LEVIATHAN to move the rig to Canal P'int. Them two side-by-side barges didn't lack much of taking up the full width of narrow Taylor Creek, but with one boat ahead and one behind, we pushed and pulled and scissor-billed them around them bends, slap down to the highway bridge at the lake. Meanwhile we had piled up enough blasted hyacinths under all them flat bottoms to leave a solid trail of verdure in our wake from the creek right spang into the Palm Beach Canal, 25 miles acrost the open lake. It seemed as how nobody had thought about measurin' the width of the bridge's openin', and we like to didn't make it through. We had to cut a-loose and warp them barges through by hand with only an inch of daylight on each side. Then, with my LEVIA-THAN lashed alongside the OSCEOLA, I j'ined the skipper in his pilot house as he laid a course for Canal P'int.

Cap'n Johnson loved to have a listener, so before we'd crossed the lake I l'arned how he had got his start when he'd come from Louisiana to Kissimmee in 1883 to help Disston raise his sugar cane, and I reckon that he done right well, for cane from his farm at Southport took top prize at the New Orleans World's Fair. Atter that for a while he run the shops which built Disston's boats and dredges. When he first came here the town wasn't nothing but the few shacks of a frontier trading post, so his first home had been a dog-trot house of logs with a leanto kitchen. Then he built hisself a big home, two and a half stories high hit was, with porches all around, down on the lake shore near the shops.

From first to last old Cap'n Clay had owned a heap of boats. His first had been the 35 foot sidewheel, MAM-IE LOWNE, a sister ship to the SCHIPMAN. Boating was right profitable, so he bought the CINCINNATI and changed her name to ROSE ADA. In 1893 he gave her a new 57 foot hull with some makeshift cabins on her upper deck, which he later taken off, and shortened the name

ROSEADA stops at Ft. Gardner to show tourists an Indian camp.
Captain Clay Johnson (right) looks on.

to ROSEADA, but she navigated the river and the big
lake to nigh onto thirty years.

This boat Clay had named for his two daughters.
Rose had got her name from her uncle, Captain R. E.
Rose, general manager for Disston, and she had
married E. P. "Lon" Dann, while Ada was the wife
of George G. Steffee. The ROSEADA was run by
George Steffee down to Bassenger as long as thar was
a dollar in it, the last boat to make this run. Then Cap'n
Johnson gave Steffee the boat and George run her on
the upper lakes ontil the hurricane in 1928 piled her up
on the beach at Kissimmee.

Hit were only a year atter he built the ROSEADA
that Cap'n Johnson built his favorite boat, the LILLIE,
named for his wife. Like most all the steamers, LILLIE

was small, but with her fancy cabins and her bang up good meals, she was give up to be the queen of all the river's passenger boats. Cap'n Johnson operated her his-self as long as she stayed on the run to Bassenger.

His last and biggest steamer, built in 1910, was the OSCEOLA, 74.6 feet long, big enough to haul 1,000 boxes of oranges and still make 12 miles an hour upstream, or at least, so I've heard tell. OSCEOLA'S first skipper had been the other son-in-law, Lon Dann, but he soon quit to run his own own ROSEADELE in competition, which didn't pleasure the old capain ary bit, but he could-n't sull forever, so in later years he pardoned Dann and even give him the LILLIE for a present. Dann used the boat for towin' on Biscayne Bay, ontil Captain Ed Forbes paid $50 for her hull to ferry vegetables from his farm on Ritta Island.

Whilst on the river the OSCEOLA had been skippered mostly by the captain's only son, "Little Clay" as he was called, full of business, and who loved to run on schedule. Atter his death, which hit the old man pow'ful hard, Captain Johnson run the OSCEOLA hisself.

In spite of competition from other steamers and them thar new-fangled gasoline propeller boats, if'n thar were something to be moved that were either difficult or heavy, old Clay was most sure to get the job. Moving sugar mills was to him almost a habit. With his MAMIE LOWNE he had brought in all the bricks and machinery for Disston's mill at St. Cloud, the first sugar mill on muck land in Fluridy. Then in 1923, for F. E. Bryant's sugar company he fotched the first mill in the Ever-glades to Canal P'int. That same year Cap'n Johnson hauled the machinery for the Pennsylvania Company's new mill at Pennsuco, sixteen miles up the canal from Miami. But when this mill was abandoned and had to be moved to the new Southern Sugar Company's location at Clewiston, he done larned that times had changed. Rail-

Power boat ROSEADELE, built by Lon Dan, skippered by Edward
Hall. She carried land seekers from Kissimmee to Micco Bluff, where
they transferred to autos to view the country.

roads had been built and they could do the haulin'
cheaper. But in between times he kept his steamers busy
haulin' building material, bridge girders, and rock and
sand for the construction of locks and for building Conners Highway. Then for variety, when the Everglades
canals would git so clogged with hyacinths till a gator
couldn't sca'cely navigate, the state used to hire the
OSCEOLA'S paddlewheel to fan the cussed things out to
sea.

Her last job was on the Palm Beach Canal, ferryin'
automobiles from Loxahatchee to Twenty Mile Bend
when the road to Belle Glade was being rebuilt. She
struck a submerged stump and sunk thar at the dairy.
The boat was under contract to the state and he could
have collected damages, but you know how Clay Johnson
was, he didn't even make a claim.

Captain Johnson's Favorite Boat, the LILLIE, Named for His Wife.
"Queen of the River's Passenger Steamers".

Cap'n Clay Johnson was a right clever hearted man, and generous as well—too generous. If'n he'd collected all his bills and bought some orange groves he might have retired a wealthy man, but he believed that life was made for livin', so let's have some fun as you go along, and it seemed that he jist loved everybody. When he was at home his big house would resound with the laughter of parties and dancing, and even on a river trip he might lay up at a landing and send out notice for a square dance. Then whilst the caller was a-calling sets and the couples sashayed on the hard packed ground, old Clay would be sawing away on his fiddle to furnish music for the frolic. Then like as not, during an intermission he might take up his flute and smoke a little tune on it. Schedules never worried the good skipper ary bit. He might hang around a landing for hours on end if'n thar was somebody thar to talk to, more especially if'n hit happened to be a lady (didn't I tell you that he loved everybody?)

Once on returning from a trip the skipper's wife exclaimed "Clay, how did you get that awful scratch across your cheek?" "Scratch? Oh, that scratch! Well you see, honey, down at Grape Hammock I picked up a right purty lady passenger, and when I tried to kiss her, why, her hatpin scratched my face!" And so, of course Miss Lilly didn't believe ary a word of it.

Now as I was a-sayin', Cap'n Johnson was a most clever and agreeable feller, but, like most skippers of his time, he could, when riled, display a most bodacious temper, and his profanity could shame the skinner of a government mule. But I don't reckon we should be too harsh in judging, son. Thar's times, they say, that try men's souls and I'll be dad burned if I don't believe that towboatin' is chuck full of them. Did you ever have a barge break loose in a sudden squall on a dead lee shore, and with nobody to make it fast again but some cow footed backwoods deckhand who didn't know a towing bitt from a bilge pump?

At such a time the good skipper might heave his cap onto the deck and loudly cry that God A'mighty had given the winds to a little boy to play with, shake his fist towards the flashin' heavens, and then hurl a handful of silver into the elements to "pay off the wind." The lake people all knowed good and well that such blasphemy was shore to be punished by a lightnin' bolt, but nothing like that ever happened. I reckon that the good Lord just considered his many virtues and sort of overlooked the matter.

One by one the steamboats on the lake had sunk or burned or been laid up. The fleets of the Gilbert brothers, Ben Franklin Hall and Fred and Conrad Menge was here no more. The BASSENGER, SUCCESS, NAOMA and

ROSEADA, the CORONA and SUWANEE no longer splashed their way across Okeechobee's waters. Only Cap'n Johnson and his OSCEOLA remained. The OSCE-OLA was the pride of his heart. He bragged that she could float in a heavy dew and out-pull anything on the lake. But when, in a contest off St. Lucie Canal, the little diesel tug, C. J. MORROW, pulled the big OSCE-OLA backwards, the old man never was the same again, then when she sunk at Loxahatchee he give up.

Steamboatin' was finished, his last boat sunk, his eyesight failin', and so, having nothing fu'ther to keep him hyar, in October of 1931, he quietly slipped his moorings for his farewell journey on the River of No Return. And that, son, was the end of steamboatin' in Fluridy.

CHAPTER FIVE

Caloosahatchee—"Beautiful River"

There used to be a river that they called Caloosahatchee, and a right pretty stream it was too, by Neds. But it aint the same river that they call Caloosahatchee now, no, not by a jugful! The present day Caloosahatchee is pretty enough in its way with oaks and cabbage trees lining its banks, and now and again an orange grove back there behind the river swamp. But what they call the Caloosahatchee nowadays, atter all the straightening, widening and deepening that's been done, is nothing more than a glorified canal in my estimation.

You know, there used to be a heap of difference in the rivers of the Everglades. Down on the East Coast there were the Miami River, the New River, Snake Creek and Snapper Creek and all the rest. They was mostly tolerably short and swift and narrow, and they knowed just where they was a-going to. The Kissimmee now, was just the opposite, long and flat and sluggish, and she could be miles wide in an overflow, but crooked? Oh good gosh, how that stream could wind around!

Now the Caloosahatchee, she was plenty crooked too, but in other ways she was a heap different from the old Kissimmee. Instead of being wide and flat, with sca'cely any high ground to be seen, the Caloosahatchee was nar-

41

row, almost like a canal, and her banks, they was high, some places ten or fifteen feet straight up when the river was low, and them banks was lined with oaks and cabbages and cypress trees, with moss hanging in long streamers from the branches, and those branches near about meeting acrost the river till it was blame near dark in daylight under them. Oh, it was a pretty sight to go up that Caloosahatchee in the old steamboating days. But the prettiest sight and the sweetest smelling part of all was to steam past all them orange groves, loaded with their yellow fruit and fragrant blossoms. Along one stretch of river was three solid miles of groves up there at Alva where Floweree had his place. I'm telling you, that Caloosahatchee was a pretty stream back then. Them land salesmen taking their wide eyed prospects up to the lake to sell them ten acres of sawgrass muck, used to say that "Caloosahatchee" was the Seminole word for "Beautiful River", and that sounded logical enough, unless you already knowed that it had been named instead

Caloosahatchee River near LaBelle.

for the Calusa Indians who had lived here long before the Seminoles. But then, them thar pink eared Yankees believed every word those salesmen spoke, and the Caloosahatchee was beautiful beyond a doubt, so I don't reckon it did no great harm what the salesmen said about the name.

Down at Ft. Myers where the steamboats docked and where them land seekers got aboard for their trip to view the "Everglades Promised Land", the river was near about to being a mile and a half wide. It stayed wide too, blamed near up to Olga, the first settlement, twelve mile upstream. Four miles further was Rialto but it weren't no town, only scattering groves, then on first one side and then the other you'd come to Caloosa, Owanita and then Alva. Alva was the main town up the river then. There was a bridge here too, a couple of hundred feet in length,

Bridge at Alva, Built in 1906. The First Bridge across the Caloosahatchee River.

which shows you how the river had narrowed down. But
from Alva on up to Ft. Thompson the river weren't much
wider than a good canal, 40 or 50 feet in places and full
of sharp bends like a cussed black snake with the cramps,
and she had a right smart of a current too. With trees so
thick along the banks till you couldn't scarcely see a
boat's length ahead sometimes, it'd take some right fast
maneuvering to miss a steamboat coming downstream
with the current, as she poked her nose out through those
trees. Some of them bends was pretty sharp, I'm telling
you, like Rope Bend between Fort Denaud and Fort
Thompson. There you'd have to send a deckhand ashore
to pass a line around a cabbage tree, then steam ahead
and back up and go ahead ag'in to get your bow around
that cross current. Oh, it took some right smart good piloting to get a steamboat up the old Caloosahatchee in
them days.

But talk about your groves, they had them on the old
Caloosahatchee, and they was money makers too. Take
D. A. G. Floweree, that moneyed cattle man from out
west, who comed here in 1902 and planted 400 acres of
citrus above Alva. When his grove wasn't but only four
years old he refused $15,000 for his crop of fruit, and
one year he shipped 83,000 boxes so I've heared tell, and
that's a heap of sweetness if you was to ask me. Some of
them old trees are there till yet, though it'd take a fifty
foot ladder for to reach their tops by now.

Then up above this grove a piece was Reynold's sawmill and then come Garvey's grove. Ft. Simmons had been
betwixt these two places in the Indian war. Then came
Ft. Denaud, named for Pierre Denaud, a French Canad-
ian, who'd traded here with the Indians before the soldiers came, and Ft. Adams used to be acrost on the north
side during the Seminole war. They called them forts, but
heck, they was nothing much but stockades of logs, with
a palmetto shack inside to house their supplies. The soldiers, they slept in tents and all hands left when the

rainy season come on. Ft. Adams had been named for an officer wounded in the Battle of Okeechobee, and Ft. Thompson, like Ft. Center on Fisheating Creek and Ft. Van Swearingen east of the lake, was named for officers killed in that same fracas.

The woods along here was powerful thick, so thick that if you stepped ashore you'd sca'cely see the sky, what with the dense growth of oaks and pines and cabbages and rubber trees all covered over with vines, and with them pretty red and green and purple airplants in their branches and moss a-fluttering from their limbs. Oh, it were a pretty sight. And fish? You could look right slam to the bottom of the river and see them fish of every kind a-darting and a-swimming till it were a plumb sight to see!

Above Ft. Denaud was LaBelle, which wasn't much of a place till Everett Goodno come along, although Cap'n Hendry had already made a start there and had laid out some streets. A Frenchman who lived thereabouts told Cap'n Hendry, "I have travelled ze world around and

Rope Bend, near Ft. Denaud.

nevair have I seen a place so bee-utiful as zis. You should call ze town LaBelle, ze Beautiful", and so he did. Now this Cap'n Francis Asbury Hendry was the local cattle king. He'd first discovered the Caloosahatchee back in the Seminole war when he'd been dispatch bearer for Cap'n Leslie's cavalry, and they'd sont him to Ft. Myers. Atter that he'd been a Confederate captain in the War Between the States. The war had sort of disrupted his cattle raising on the Alafia River, but after hostilities was over he moved his cow critters south of the Caloosahatchee in 1870, to where cattle hadn't never been grazed before. Here he had 30,000 acres of land and was doing right well, buying whole herds from others and shipping them to Cuba along with his own, and getting scandalous rich. But when the War with Spain come to an end, so did the Cuban cattle market, but then, by Neds, Captain Hendry's I.O.U.'s for herds he'd bought began to coming due.

Hit were about this time that Everett E. Goodno, with his mother, comed here from Kansas. Goodno, he liked

A Home on the Caloosahatchee.

Ft. Myers but his mother didn't want to live in town. He hadn't never married, so his mother was his boss. He explored up the river and the futher up he went the better hit looked to him, so he up and bought a few thousand acres from Cap'n Hendry, including the townsite of La-Belle, which got that gentleman out of his financial bog. Cap'n Hendry then moved to Ft. Myers and got political, serving in the state legislature and the senate and on the city commission. In course of time he even helped to get a new county carved off from Lee, and so they went and named it Hendry County.

Everett Goodno, he begun to do about and promote his new town of La Belle. He built a hotel thar by the river, the only hotel, excusing the Bolles Hotel at Ritta, betwixt Ft. Myers and West Palm Beach, and he named the hotel for hisself, the Everett. It takened him three years to get the hotel built, but hit were kept busy atter it was finished, with all them land company boats taking prospects to the lake. La Belle was the upriver trading post, with two or three stores, a blacksmith shop and a bridge acrost the river. The blacksmith, Porter Dean, he doubled as bridge tender. La Belle soon got to be a right peart little town.

A couple of miles above La Belle was old Ft. Thompson. That's where the droves of cattle used to cross the river on their way to Punta Rassa where they was loaded onto ships for Cuba. Ft. Thompson oncet was the most important place on all the upper river. Now, don't get me wrong. Ft. Thompson wasn't any town. Shucks, it never was a settlement, not even in the boating days. Hit were the head of the river. In olden days there'd been a high waterfall here where a rock ledge come to the surface, damming all the water coming down from Lake Okeechobee and making it spread out above to form Lake Flirt. When Disston had decided to open up the river to Lake Okeechobee, Cap'n Fred Menge had blasted out them falls in 1881, and that left a quarter mile of rapids here in a bend. Hit used to be a terrible place to get through in that narrow rocky channel when the water was low. Sometimes a boat got stuck and had to use a winch to get ahead, but in going upstream a steamboat had some advantages for she pushed the water ahead which give her a little more to float in. But in 1909, atter the state took over drainage operations, the big dredge CALOOSAHATCHEE cleaned out them rapids good and proper, and then most any boat could go up to Lake Okeechobee, fish boats, land company boats and sportsmen, too, even the big barges which brung up oil for the dredges on the lake.

Hit was then that Goodno built his ice plant at Ft. Thompson, a might queer place for an ice plant, you may think, but those Okeechobee catfish boats needed ice, and Goodno made $1000 a month selling ice when the catfishing was good. The ice plant stood in the prairie 100 yards back from the river, but a tram car on a wooden trestle carried the ice cakes down to the boat. In this prairie, to

LaBelle. Everett Hotel. Bridge at Left.

the eastward, was all that remained of the old fort, just the stumps of the heart pine palisades where somebody had oncet cut them down to get the logs. The stumps remained there, too, still unrotted, until the government straightened out the river when it started to build the Hoover Dike around the lake.

About 100 feet back from the ice plant was the old home of Cap'n Hendry, a two story house on a little mound near the edge of the hammock, unfinished and unpartitioned inside, but yet a right good house for its day and time.

Goodno, not satisfied with having a hotel at La Belle, built another one, the Ft. Thompson Park Hotel, in the hammock near the old Hendry house, which Goodno hisself now lived in. This new hotel hit was reserved for big shots and VIP's like Henry Ford and Edison and such. It was Goodno who got these two to plant the nearby prairies in golden rod in later years, trying to find a substitute for rubber. They made rubber alright, but hit were

Entrance to Ft. Thompson Park Hotel.

too blamed expensive and so they give it up. But Ford bought the Everett Hotel in 1924 and changed the name to Riverview. The hotel burned down in 1954, but long before that the Ft. Thompson Hotel had been torn down, the ice plant closed when fish boats quit running from the lake, the old Hendry house burned in the 1930's and nothing now remains of Ft. Thompson excusing only the ice machinery's concrete base and the mound where Hendry's house once stood.

And that, my boy, was the Caloosahatchee in the old steamboating days. From Ft. Thompson slap on up to Lake Okeechobee the way was through flat open country, canals, and shallow lakes and drowned out prairies, with sometimes pines and hammocks way off in the distance. First you'd come to Lake Flirt, about five mile by two. They say as how hit got that name from the army's topsail schooner named FLIRT which had fotched some Injun chasing soldiers up the river. This was the same FLIRT which had been on the Keys when Dr. Perrine and them was massacreed. In the boating days the hammocks hereabouts had been famous for their turkeys and their deer, and the lake for hits ducks and pink curlews. Some of these pink spoonbills must have survived, for Fred Flanders, the state's engineer, he seed a few feeding here several times about in 1940. He found something else here too. Atter this Lake Flirt had dried up, there was found a most bodacious collection of old fossil bones of dinosaurs and all them old timey critters, and mammoth's teeth as big as a cow man's hat. Flanders allowed as how this must have been a bog during prehistoric times, sort of like the La Brea Tar Pits in California. He given all them bones and shells to the National Park Service, he says, but don't be surprised if'n you see a whopping big bone or vertebra hanging in some Cracker's porch thereabouts.

From Lake Flirt a canal led through that well named Lettuce Lake and on to Bonnet Lake, full of water bonnets and weeds. Then come Reedy Canal, a five mile mess of cattails and moss. On its north side, near Bonnet Lake was that famous Coffee Mill Hammock, nothing but a dozen cabbage trees behind a steep rock bank, but this were a favorite place for boatmen to tie up when darkness come down, for you couldn't run those shoal and unmarked channels in the lakes at night. Buried in this hammock was the remains of a man named Atkins who had been shot at Sugarberry Hammock and came floating down the canal. The hammock, so they say, got its name from a hand coffee mill which had been nailed to one of them cabbage trees by some long forgotten cow hunter, nobody knows when. At any rate hit had that name in Disston's day. Some of them cabbage trees are still growing there till yet, near Ortona Locks.

Reedy Canal led into Lake Hicpochee, five miles wide by six or seven long and surrounded by a sawgrass marsh.

The route for the canal from Ft. Thompson to Lake Hicpochee, through all them lakes and sawgrass marshes,

Coffee Mill Hammock. "A Dozen Cabbage Trees Behind a Steep Rock Bank."

had first been laid out by the two old cattle kings, Jacob Summerlin and F. A. Hendry, who knowed this country better than most anybody else. At their own expense they got a crew, and they waded mud and slashed through head high sawgrass for days on end to set up flags for the dredge to follow. Old Jake Summerlin was then near about sixty years of age.

Although for politness Hicpochee was called a lake, in the boating days hit weren't nothing but a thin skim of water spread over bottomless soup-doodle muck. Boatmen, when crossing it, would pump their engine's cooling water from their bilge if'n they'd forgot to fotch an extra can of water along. Oncet there had been a dam at the lake's lower end to prevent Okeechobee's water from flooding the groves down river, but hit had been blowed out in 1903. Disston had dug a stub canal on each

Steamer SUWANEE entering Three Mile Canal from Lake Okeechobee. The City of Moore Haven now Surronds this old Flat Top Cypress.

side of this here lake. The mile long Woodyard Canal to pine timber was for to git fuel for his dredge, while, on the east side, the Nine Mile Canal to Sand Point, was for hauling firewood to the dredge in Ritta River. But the main channel from Hicpochee to Lake Okeechobee was Three Mile Canal. Here Lon Woodhull's tin fishing shack was, in 1908, the only building between Ft. Thompson and the big lake.

Where Three Mile Canal j'ined Lake Okeechobee was the only landmark there were for miles around in all that sawgrass marsh. The old Flat Top Cypress, with lake water lapping at hits roots, marked the entrance to the canal, and hit were a famous landmark in the catfishing days for sure. A steamboat pilot coming from acrost the lake might first sight tall Hoopskirt Cypress at Liberty Point, with its base draped with moonvines growing over elder bushes, but thar wasn't no mistaking the tree at Three Mile Canal, with hits top as flat as if whacked off by a giant machete, and with an empty barrel nailed up in its branches.

But now the town of Moore Haven has the tree surrounded, and hit's a good seven mile out the old channel to the open lake. The runboats has quit and the steamboats are long gone, a town has grown up where the lake waters oncet rolled, other trees overshadows hit in the city park, but old Flat Top is still standing thar till yet, just as she was when Jake Summerlin marked out the route for the canal. And I reckon, buddy, from the way she looks, with her new spring crop of green, that she may be thar for a right smart long time to come.

CHAPTER SIX

Smoke Boats on the Caloosahatchee

Back in them days when Hamilton Disston was doing about at Kissimmee, bringin' in settlers and making business for the steamboats, there was blamed little happenin' here on the Caloosahatchee. Excusin' for a few scatterin' settlers and some cow men here and yonder, there wasn't nothin' much here on this river but the little village of Ft. Myers. Steamboats sometimes come down from Punty Gorda where Plant's railroad ended, but shucks, hit were 55 water miles to Ft. Myers and not sca'cely worth the trip.

What really started things to poppin' here on the river, son, were nothin' more nor less than that bodacious Big Freeze on February 5, 1895, when citrus trees was killed all over Fluridy. When word got around that on the Caloosahatchee the settlers' dooryard trees hadn't even lost their fruit, that, my boy, was when the boom began. Froze-out grove owners from up state and moneyed visitors from the north flocked here and started clearin' land and plantin' orange trees like mad. Of course, there was no roads here them days, only sandy trails through the woods, so when them oranges matured they had to be hauled by boat. At first they went to Punty Gorda, but when the railroad was extended into Ft.

Myers, in 1904 hit were, that town become a busy river port, and a heap more so when all them prospective settlers and speculators begun a-flockin' to Lake Okeechobee to see the "Everglades Promised Land".

Them was the days of steamboats on the river, my boy, and the king bees of this river was the brothers, J. Fred and Conrad Menge. If'n you seed ary a steamboat above Ft. Myers, she likely belonged to them. If she didn't then, she would before so very long. Yes, the king bees of the river trade was Fred and "Carnie" Menge. Cap'n J. Fred Menge now, he was a big husky man who always stood so straight and tall, rared back like as if he was a-lookin' at somethin' fur away. He'd been the superintendent for Disston's dredgin' work, yet whilst he

Captain J. Fred Menge (left), and Captain Bill Murray.

were a-dredgin' in them swamps and glades, he taken time off to do a bit of courtin'. He up and married Virginia Lee Hendry, daughter of Cap'n Francis Asbury Hendry, the Ft. Thompson cattle king, which I don't reckon hurt Cap'n Fred's financial standin' much, for whensomever he quit Disston he up and bought the little steamers GOPHER and MAMIE for to take out fishing parties in the Gulf.

Now, on the Caloosahatchee, the first smoke boat to make regular runs up that river had been the ANNAH C. She'd been built by Charles Dudley, though I wouldn't doubt he might have had some backing from John L. Wilhelm, for first off, he hauled lumber from Wilhelm's sawmill at Denaud to his finishing mill on Twelve Mile Crick. This crick's name was changed to Orange River later on, but hit's the same stream where the Menges had their boat ways and shops and hit run on up to Buck-

ANAH C. in the Orange River. She was the First Steamer to Make Regular Trips up the Caloosahatchee.

in'ham. The Menges bought the ANNAH C and put her to haulin' oranges, then they bought the CITY OF ATHENS from the Gilberts up Kissimmee way. She had burned and sunk at Ft. Thompson, but the Menges run her for a right smart longer ontil she burned up sure enough about fifteen years later.

That Fred and Carnie Menge, they was steamboat men from the heart. They kept right on a-buyin' boats and haulin' oranges and carryin' passengers, too. They owned the 100 foot steamer UNEEDA which could tote 2300 boxes of oranges at one load, the GREY EAGLE, which run the river for many years, until, old and rotten, she was laid up near Orange River, and her

CITY OF ATHENS at Captain Hendry's home at Ft. Thompson. After She Sunk for the Second Time at Ft. Thompson, in 1915 Capt. Hendry Converted her Paddlewheel into an Irrigation Pump for His Orange Grove. The Paddlewheel being Turned by the River's Current.

Menge's UNEEDA in 1910. "She could tote 2300 Boxes of Oranges".

Menge Brothers' THOMAS A. EDISON in the Caloosahatchee.

machinery was put into the UNEEDA. Besides these, they owned the steel hulled R A L P H   B A R K E R, which run to Buckingham, and the launches RIVER-SIDE, SEMINOLE and TITANIC, and the fifty foot propeller boat NYANZA. Then they owned the old CORONA which had been built by Cap'n Ben F. Hall at Alva and which Cap'n Peter Cone in later days put to haulin freight on Okeechobee Lake. But I reckon that about the finest of all their boats were the passenger packet THOMAS A. EDISON. She'd been built in 1904 at Apalachicola, drawed only 2½ feet light, and be-sides her passengers, could haul 1200 boxes of oranges. She were a beauty of a boat, but she come to a right sad end. On the night of January 30, 1914, with a full load of fruit, she were tied up at the Lee County Packing House. That were the night when the packin' house ketched afire, and hit and some neighborin' buildings burned slap to the ground. The same wind which fanned the fire had lowered the river. The EDISON were hard and fast aground and all the tugboats couldn't budge her

POINSETTIA at Okeechobee City, after part of her cabin had been removed to lighten her draft. Even so, it took the Halls three months to get her from Ft. Myers, around Cape Sable to Ft. Lauderdale and Lake Okeechobee.

a-loose, and that were the last of the THOMAS A. EDISON.

I said that the Menge brothers had most of the river business, but they didn't have hit all. Runnin' the lower river and to Punty Gorda there were the Plant company's big two stacker ST. LUCIE, run by Cap'n Fisher, Cap'n Kinzie's BELLE OF MYERS and FREE LANCE, Cap'n Bill White's little ALICE HOWARD and the steam-propeller boat GLADYS, and Stanton's twin stacked excursion boat POINSETTIA. Cap'n Ben F. Hall, with his brother Edward H. and Ben's son Ed, they bought the POINSETTIA at government auction and allowed as how they'd take her up to the big lake for to haul catfish there, but I reckon if'n they'd a-knowed what they was a-gettin' into, they'd have kept their money in the bank. The lake was about at hits lowest stage. They couldn't get up the Caloosahatchee, so they fotched her clear

Captain Benjamin Franklin Hall, Jr. (kneeling), with two boys of his son Captain Edward H. Hall, Jr. Standing is Capt. Ben's brother Edward H. Hall, Sr.

around to Ft. Lauderdale and up the North New River
Canal. She was too wide for the locks and too deep for
the canal. They had to dam the canal and they takened
out spillways at the locks, but then bless goodness, when
they got to South Bay they had to deepen the channel
blamed near to Ritta Island. By using three barges for
pontoons they raised her enough finally to get her into
water deep enough to float. Hit takened them three solid
months of steady work to get that smoke boat here from
from Ft. Myers to the lake. Then, bless Pete, they found
that they couldn't make her pay, until at last, they found
a way to get their money back. She had cost them $5000
at the sale, but they sold her to Warren for $7500 for to
become a clam digging dredge at Caxambas. So when the

Menge Brothers' UNEEDA steaming up the Caloosahatchee.

lake got high they delivered her, and she finally sunk at Beautiful Island in the Caloosahatchee above Ft. Myers.

There was other steamers on the Caloosahatchee which didn't belong to the Menges. Up the river, the Floweree grove had hits own sternwheelers, NORMA and FLOWEREE, powered by heavy duty gasoline engines. Homer Hand at La Belle built the 65 foot HOMER HAND which run to Tantie and which finally burned at Bonita Springs. Oscar Hand bought Cap'n Tom Bass' launch CHINDY, lengthened her and renamed her REX-ALL, and she were the fastest thing on the river. And then there was Cap'n W. H. (Bill) Towles, who owned the sternwheeler MILDRED and the sidewheel PLANT-ER.

SUCCESS as she looked while owned by Harmon Raulerson. After she burned in Ft. Myers Captain Bass made her longer and wider, and installed new engines and water tube boiler. He sold her to Kenzie Brothers for hauling barges of shell from Captiva Island to Ft. Myers. She was then sold to Ben Johnson Dredging Company to tow oil to his dredges in Indian Prairie Canal, then to Dave Ireland and to Harmon Raulerson, then to John Ringling.

And, oh yes, I musn't forget the sternwheeler SUC-CESS. She'd been built in Kissimmee in 1906, but she run mostly on the Caloosahatchee, and she were the last smoke boat to run that river. Fifty-six foot by 14.5 she were when she were built, and only 2.7 foot draft. Cap'n Tom A. Bass got to be the biggest catfish man on Lake Okeechobee, but he started out with the SUCCESS, hauling fish to Ft. Myers from his camps on the big lake. Hit were while on one of these trips to town, in October of 1907, the SUCCESS ketched afire and burned. Cap'n Ed Hall, he were her skipper, but he was ashore right then, and so he lost all his clothes, some money and a right fine rifle too.

Her hull, hit weren't burned too bad, and so Cap'n Bass rebuilt hit five foot longer, two foot wider, and put

Captain Edward H. Hall, Jr. Son of Captain Benjamin Franklin Hall. Taken in Okeechobee City while all dressed up for Sunday.

her to hauling catfish once more until he sold her to Kinsey brothers in 1908. Dave Ireland owned her for a while, then Harmon Raulerson from Okeechobee, who had her hauling tomatoes from the lake in 1924, and bringing pilings up the Kissimmee for the bridge at Bassenger. Then John Ringling, the circus man, bought her for towing on a causeway job from Sarasota to an island in the Gulf, till she sank and was abandoned at Siesta Key in 1933.

The old SUCCESS, she were the last wet tail boat to run the Caloosahatchee, but from first to last there was a plumb slush of smoke boats on this river. And them steamboat skippers, they was held in respect by all the folks ashore, envied by the boys and admired by all the girls. The most famous I reckon was Cap'n Fred Menge and Cap'n Ben F. Hall, maybe because they could cuss so bodaciously. Some few skippers, like Conrad Menge and Perry Hull, and Cap'n Ben's son Edward H. Hall, carried both master's and engineer's certificates so's they could "run both ends of the boat". That Cap'n Ed Hall, now, he

Steamer GLADYS at Ft. Myers.

didn't go ashore when steamboating played out. He went to sea, was in both World Wars and the Korean fracas and just retired as Commander in the merchant marine, and now he's writing a book too, about his experiences and about steamboats he's known on this big lake and on the Atlantic Ocean as well. He's given me a powerful lot of help on this'un for which I thank him.

There was Cap'n Prince who brought the SUWAN-NEE here, Cap'n Moyer of the CONSTITUTION, Jimmie Cochran of the JUANITA, Nick Armeda, captain of the THOMAS A. EDISON and one of the sharpest pilots on the river, Robert Dupree of the old GREY EAGLE, and the brothers Charlie and Bill Murray. Their brother Fred, and Charlie's son Earl, were engineers, and another engineer, Cleve Hicks, now caretaker at Ortona Cemetery, who says he has been engineer or fireman on blamed near every steamer which ever ran the river.

Menge's Steel Hulled RALPH BARKER

Oh, there was no lack of steamboats on the Caloosahatchee, and propeller boats, too, in time. But all of them didn't run up to Lake Okeechobee. The first really big boat to run from Ft. Myers to the lake you know, were the big BERTHA LEE, and you'll recollect that hit takened Cap'n Ben F. Hall 52 days to get up to Kissimmee, and that were in 1883. The next passenger boat to try this route was not till 1891 when Hamilton Disston, in the steamer named for him, taken a few friends on up to Kissimmee for to see if'n hit might be a payin' passenger run. I reckon it didn't seem a smart idea, for it weren't till 1906 that we hear of another big boat makin' this trip. Hit were endurin' that winter that Cap'n Fred Menge made some excursion trips to Lake Okeechobee in his SUWANEE, the first big boat to go up the river to the lake in five whole blessed years.

But hit were at about this time that catfish began to comin' from the lake, so Cap'n Bill Towles started runnin' to Tantie (what's Okeechobee City now) in his steamers PLANTER and MILDRED and so did the Hand brothers in their HOMER HAND and REXALL, carryin' up supplies and fetchin' catfish back and there was the motor boat NORTH STAR which run betwixt Moore Haven and Tantie, hauling freight.

Hit were here in Tantie, too, that one steamer was built, though she started out by being a gas-propeller boat. Henry H. Hancock had her built in 1909 and named her SERENA VICTORIA, for his mother, a fifty foot by twelve foot job, with two engines and two 24" propellers. Sam Grey, who built her, tells me that she could make 16 miles an hour, and could haul 325 boxes of oranges. The trip to Ft. Myers took only fourteen hours going down and sixteen coming back. Now, 325 boxes of oranges might seem a puny load, but before that, them Tantie folks had been hauling them to Ft. Pierce by ox cart, taking 30 boxes to a load, a trip of seven days. But atter a while, Hancock, not satisfied with a good thing, had Sam Grey and Ed Hall take out those engines and install the machinery and paddle wheel from the NAOMA III, but then she was under-powered and never did much after that.

By the winter of 1912-13 there was so many settlers along the river and so many oranges too, that the Menges started makin' daily trips from Ft. Myers to Olga, Rialto, Caloosa, Owanita and LaBelle with their glass cabin boats ADA MAY and DAWN, and with the steamers UNEEDA and THOMAS A. EDISON, to boot. The CORONA, she sailed each Tuesday from LaBelle to Citrus Center and across the lake to Okeechobee City up Taylor Creek. Menge's literature allowed as how this creek was a magnificent stream, "a perfect paradise, the hunter's and fisherman's dream, the Seminole's Happy Hunting Ground". Sometimes the CORONA would even go fifty miles up the "magnificent Kissimmee River" to Ft. Bassenger. Her staterooms, they said, were "thoroughly screened", I reckon they needed to be, and she could take sixteen passengers, and she had "toilets with hot and cold water, and meals A No. 1", which was luxury travel to be sure. Hit were in this same winter of 1912-13 that the canal was opened from Lauderdale to the lake and that were the beginnin' of real boat traffic up to Okeechobee Lake. Bolles and all them other promoters of Everglades lands started bringin' their prospects on this cross state trip to show them those oceans of wet sawgrass where they could get rich on ten acre tracts. Charlie Murray in Bolles' QUEEN OF THE GLADES fotched a many a land seeker on these trips. Fred Menge was makin' weekly cross state runs in the SUWANEE and so was Cap'n Moore in his WANDERLUST. Then, from Ft. Lauderdale, Cap'n Felix Forbes was runnin' twice weekly trips to the lake in his MINDINAO where the passengers was transferred to his MAYFLOWER to continue down the river. All these passengers spent a night at one of the hotels at Ritta, (what we call Lake Harbor now). Forbes charged $9.50 for the two day trip or $15 if'n you went both ways.

As time went on and more settlers come here to the lake, the Menges run their launches ADA MAY and DAWN slam on up to Ritta, and so did Cap'n Moore's wife in the EVA while he doubled in the WANDER-LUST.

Now, let me tell you about that WANDERLUST, son, she sure were a long lived boat, a 40 foot glass cabin boat with a three cylinder Standard engine, and she'd been built in Ft. Myers in 1909. Cap'n Moore run her to the lake on scheduled runs for a right smart number of years, but sometimes she'd make an excursion, like for instance, the one he made in July 1913 when she was chartered by the crew of the dredge CALOOSAHATCHEE which were a-diggin' in the Hillsboro Canal. The dredge boys fotched up their girl friends from Ft. Lauderdale to Deer-field, then in the WANDERLUST they cruised up the ca-

WANDERLUST at Ft. Myers. "A Powerful Long Lived Boat."

nal, acrost the lake and down the river. They went on a fishin' trip in the Gulf, was entertained by the folks in Ft. Myers and La Belle and had a right fine time, and if'n no romances resulted from that trip, by Neds, I'll say they sure passed up a wallopin' good chance.

Cap'n Moore sold the WANDERLUST to Larry Crabtree, an engineer and machinist in Lauderdale. He put her to towin' barges in the construction of the Overseas Highway and other work down on the Keys, where she was run by some South Bay boys, Carl Lockmiller, Max Harrelle and Ivan Van Horn. After seven years on the Keys, Larry installed a four cylinder 40 HP Frisbie, and run her hisself as a harbor tug in Port Everglades. After she's seen steady service for forty years, when he junked her in 1949, he found her natural bent madeira frames was still as sound as on the day that she'd been built.

But there was another boat that lasted mighty long, yes, a heap longer than the WANDERLUST you might say, if'n you don't want to get too technical. This here

Menge's DAWN, which ran from Ft. Myers to Ritta

boat were the steamer SUWANEE, built in Branford, fifty mile up the Suwannee River, for T. A. Wallace. That was back in 1888, and she was brought to Ft. Myers about in 1902 or '03 by Cap'n Prince, an Englishman. Her hull was 70 feet by 16.5 and she drawed a whoppin' four foot four. The Menges bought the old wet-tail smoke boat, rebuilt her complete and put ten staterooms on her upper deck. It seems as if she'd been rebuilt so many times, that Cleve Hicks, her engineer, claims that by 1908 only one of her original timbers remained.

Before the railroad come to Ft. Myers the SUWANEE used to steam up Charlotte Harbor to Punty Gorda where she would pick up parties of them moneyed sportsmen from the north who'd come in their private railroad cars. She made a many an excursion trip of a few days or even weeks along the Gulf and later to the big lake. She was most generally always run by Cap'n Prince or Fred or Carnie Menge or maybe by Bill Murray.

After the Lauderdale canal was opened the SUWANEE started running slap acrost the state. Every

Steamer SUWANEE at Bolles Hotel at Ritta, Winter of 1912-13

Thursday she'd leave Ft. Myers to steam up the river and spend the night at Ritta on the big lake. Next day she'd go down the canal to Lauderdale and through the inland waterway to Miami. The SUWANEE only ran by day so's them touristers could see the sights, and no wonder, for her advertising proclaimed "This route can not be described. It is beyond description. The beauties are untold. The wild bird and game life has not been mentioned. The hunting is the best in the Union. The Seminole still lurks in the forests abounding this route. It is a wilderness stretching for two hundred miles from Gulf to Ocean. No where else in America can such scenes be viewed except from the deck of the Steamer SUWANEE". Yes, and all this—a week's round trip with meals and stateroom too, for a measly $25. Golly, aren't you sorry now that you never made this trip?

Most every winter the SUWANEE was chartered by

Steamer SUWANEE as she is today.
Photo by courtesy of Henry Ford Museum, Dearborn, Michigan.

Thomas A. Edison. He loved to fish, but more'n likely whilst his friends was off a-huntin' deer and turkeys in the hammocks, Edison might be a settin' thar on deck, a-dreamin' up some new invention.

The SUWANEE sunk one time in Orange River with 984 boxes of oranges aboard, but she was raised and ran again till about 1920, when she sunk once more and was abandoned at Moore Haven, and the big storm in 1926 like to have finished her for sure. But Henry Ford, the friend of Edison, got Conrad Menge to rebuild the old sternwheeler, install the engines and machinery from the THOMAS A. EDISON, and ship her to Detroit. Now, with two stacks and an open sight-seeing deck in place of all them staterooms, she's a-carryin' touristers on a lake in Henry Ford's Greenfield Village. So you see, the old SUWANEE has been rebuilt again, and this time without ary a one of her original timbers, and by now she's even got a brand new set of boilers too, but yet, by gum, I reckon that you can say she's still the Caloosahatchee's old SUWANEE.

Oscar Hand's RHORER, 1914.

CHAPTER SEVEN

New River's Whirlpools

The first surge of land seekers who came to view the
"fabulous Everglades", "as fertile as the valley of the
Nile", and who hoped to "prosper on ten acres" of sawgrass muck, had to come to Lake Okeechobee from Ft.
Myers. To be sure, at that time about all you could see of
the Everglades was some custard apple swamp, and the
Bolles Hotel and Callahan's garden at Ritta. But after
boats were allowed to use the North New River Canal,
these land prospects could traverse its length and really
see some sawgrass, yes brother, they could really see
some sawgrass! A heap of these folks now set out from
Ft. Lauderdale, and after a night at Ritta, landed in Ft.
Myers.

A lake bound boat with its crowd of wide eyed touristers—derby hatted men and long skirted ladies in their
wide brimmed hats—after leaving Lauderdale's docks
and passing through the railroad bridge, would steam
around the many tree-bordered curves of New River, a
right pretty stream, for sure. Later on, during the Boom
Days, the chamber of commerce tried to re-name the
river Himmarshee Hatchee, but the old time Seminole
name had been Coontie Hatchee, named for the fern-
like starch plant which used to grow so plentifully here
in these piney woods.

Demonstration Garden of A. V. Callahan at Ritta, 1912. This was
probably the first Vegetable Farm on the Lake Shore.

Those land seekers would be plumb amazed when
their salesman told them that this was the deepest river
for its length in all of Florida, or maybe he'd say in
the whole wide world, if'n he was feeling right extra
good that morning. He'd tell them that it was forty feet
deep and only eight miles long, and how the Indians
said that the river had appeared full grown over night.
Then he'd say as how there was a place upstream so
deep that no bottom had ever been found, and also, down
at Tarpon Bend it was all of ninety feet, and how, if
ever a man fell into the river, he was certain to be drowned. These tales, I'll have you know, all were partly true,
and it's a blamed poor salesman, I reckon, who can't be
enthusiastic about his subject.

As the boat cruised up the river these visitors might
be entranced to see their first Seminoles, wearing their
gorgeous, many-striped dress, their dugout canoes drawn
up on the sandy beach above Bryan's hotel. Then there'd

be the machine shop of Jimmy Ducane, a former circus acrobat. He'd play pool all day, a cigar perched under his long moustache. Then at night he'd run his lathe until he'd earned $20 clear, for being a batchelor, that was all he needed. He was a stomped down good machinist though.

Beyond, on a point of land where the North Fork branched off, there'd been a fort during the Indian war, but now there was the big marine railway of the Norwegian, Sigurd Dillevig, a master craftsman, for sure, who'd served his time as carpenter, painter and machinist before starting one of Lauderdale's first boat yards. This same yard I ran for him during the Boom and the Prohibition days, hauling out the finest yachts, and Coast Guard patrol and picket boats too, as well as Bimini rum runners which frequently desired to have their appearance changed, and I was here in the hurricane of '26.

Looking Upriver from Ft. Lauderdale's Highway Bridge. Catfish Runboats and Fish Houses at Left. Barge loaded with Fish Barrels near Railroad Bridge. Lake Passenger Boats at Right.

Ft. Lauderdale Waterfront in 1911. Left to Right — Restaurant, Stranahan Store (above), Unfinished Wheeler Building, destroyed by Fire with many other buildings June 2, 1912. Dade County Bank (center), W. H. Marshall Real Estate Building behind Boat Shed.

A little farther up the river the land salesman might call attention to the swanky houseboat of the famous actor, Joseph Jefferson, tied up to the bank. From here on, scarcely a building was to be seen, only just a tomato packing house now and again, nothing else but trees crowding the water's edge, but a prettier river you'd scarcely ever see. And they'd pass the only island in the river, made by cutting across the neck of a sharp U bend, and dug by Governor Broward himself when he began the drainage of the Everglades.

Above here a piece, in a bend, and just beyond the present Seaboard Railway bridge, the river widened to a round basin, all hemmed in by tall trees. A tomato packing house stood at its south edge. And here, in this basin, I'm telling you brother, the river seemed to go hog wild. This is where Old Master had pulled the plug from the river's bottom. Sometimes wild eddies, gaping skyward, chased themselves about like kittens playing tag. At other times the passengers might gaze open mouthed as the whole pool circled round and round. Floating leaves or branches, drawn toward its center, would whirl dizzily and vanish down the vortex. Here, even the biggest boat, avoiding the pool's center, was slowed and thrown off course, while water in its wake spouted and bubbled as if boiling over a fire.

This was the Whirlpool, that fearsome Whirlpool, a scary place for sure. Town folks used to tell how the old Seminole, Crop Eared Charley, in his dugout canoe with a push pole but no paddle, had been caught by the current, which whirled him round and round for hours. I reckon he'd have starved to death or else been sucked down in the eddy, if "Dutch" and Frank Marshall hadn't happened along in their motor boat.

Some oldtime boatmen recollect this whirlpool as one huge current circling like water pouring down a drain, a whirling saucer, its center five or more feet lower than its edge. There was enough slope anyway, as Frede Aunapu well recalls, that an empty gas drum on the deck of a small barge was tipped over. Once while trying to cross the pool, Aunapu's boat was slowed down by the current while the stern end of his heavily loaded barge was sucked under until water poured inside. He had to beach the barge and pump her out. At another time the current carried his boat and barge twice around the pool before he could pull away, but Max Harrelle tells that with two bages in tow, he was held by the pool for two hours.

Ed Hammer, a boatman and one of the first settlers at Davie, thinks that the pool was at its worst in 1915, '16 and '17. During those years he was towing for the dredge digging the Dania Cutoff Canal. Often he couldn't pull his barges through the pool at all and another boat would be sent from the dredge to help. At that time, so he says, instead of one, there might be several whirling funnels, each three or four feet across. There was no telling how deep those funnels were, and he sure as heck didn't want to find out. He knows of at least one small boat which capsized there, in which a man named Harper was drowned. Some folks think that there may have been others lost here too. Ed Saar, another of those early Davie boatmen, can tell you of some unpleasant adventures in this old whirlpool too.

Now for a fact, the Indians claimed that New River had showed up over night. Tony Tommie told me that his grandmother, camped in Cooley Hammock, had been there when it happened, but I'm afraid the Seminoles are wrong, for early maps show this river plain as day. But this whirlpool itself could have originated all at once, and here's the reason why. Underneath all of Florida is limestone rock which has channels underground. Sometimes the roof caves in, and that's what has caused all those "sinks" or pot holes up the state. One, near Orlando, 100 feet across and 30 feet deep appeared only a few years ago and nobody saw it happen. So this whirl-

Beautiful New River

pool could have been a hole in the roof of some underground stream. New River was fed by runoff from the Everglades. After the two big canals were dug, one of which tapped Lake Okeechobee, a heap more water came pouring down, which in flood times poured out like a torrent, and a right good share of it vanished down the whirlpool.

There were some other whirlpools in New River too. One was near its mouth, in Tarpon Bend at Cooley Hammock, where King's Creek came in. Byrd King, his sister, Mrs. Bloxam Cromartie and Mrs. Stranahan too, all agree that at one time this was the worst. Captain Ed. King had tried to fathom it, using some plumb bobs for a weight. The current snatched 200 feet of line though his hands but he never could say that he touched bottom. Later on, bottom here was found at 90 feet. Another nice whirlpool was a bit upriver from this bend, in front of Frank Stranahan's "Pioneer House" where the highway tunnel is today. Mrs. Stranahan tells me that the downrushing water could make enough commotion to wake people sleeping upstairs. Sometimes she'd go out to see if the noise was caused by her horse falling into the river. When a sea wall was built along the river's edge, they had to bridge this spot with railroad irons.

Now, where did the water go that vanished down these whirlpools? Off shore from Port Everglades there used to be a fresh water spring surging upward in the sea. I reckon that it was fed by some underground channel from the river. This stands to reason too. Those early Davie boatmen learned that the big whirlpool upriver was always worst when the tide was low at sea, and often they'd tie up their boats and wait till it subsided.

When I first came to Lauderdale, town folks used to brag that this Whirlpool up river was bottomless. Later on they cooled off and claimed that it was 110 feet in depth. It was about in 1924 that I decided to find out if this was true, although by that time the pool was no longer whirling. About halfway between its north side and the center, and using a house jack for a weight, I found it to be forty-one feet to bottom. I didn't try the middle for my mother was with me in the launch. She was so frightened by all the stories that she'd heard, till she was nearly frantic.

In 1939 the U. S. Engineers made soundings in New River. They found twenty-two pot holes in its bottom, but at that time the deepest was only 37.3 feet, and this was exactly in the same place I'd sounded. The old pool quit its whirling about the time of World War I, when the Lake and Glades were low. It never whirled again although we've had floods since then a-plenty.

So what do you reckon caused the old pool to quit its devilment? Pardner, I wouldn't know, though Lord knows I've tried to learn the reason. But here's a likely story, though I wouldn't even swear that it's the explanation. Captain Louis L. Dodge, with his tug GLOBE, had been fetching boulders from the banks of North New River Canal for to build a sea wall in town. On one trip his barge, overloaded and most likely leaking too, was sucked down here and sunk. The barge with its tons of rock could have sealed up the cavern's opening, then sand and muck washed down from the canals near about finished filling up the hole. Anyway, nowadays the whirlpool is plumb forgot, but brother, when she was working at her trade she surely was a dilly.

Above the whirlpool a piece, the lake bound boat would turn into the North New River canal, but further up the river a bit was the South Canal. Here, at the river's head, in olden times there'd been a waterfall. When water in the river and the Glades was low it made a drop of several feet, but if the Glades were wet you'd hardly notice it at all. Ringed round with ferns and moss and cypress trees, and with fish cavorting in the clear water, this was a picnic spot for those early settlers in Ft. Lauderdale. New River was a beautiful stream from mouth to source. Even today, though fine homes have changed the looks a heap, it still is, for that matter. But mister, nowadays you'll have to search the city and the whole blamed countryside to find a person who's ever heard tell of the whirlpools in New River.

CHAPTER EIGHT

That Terrible North Canal

Any song about the joys of boating on Lake Okeechobee should by rights have a verse on the North New
River Canal, so we will label this stanza "The North
Canal Blues". For a right smart number of years this
waterway was the main avenue of traffic between the
big lake and civilization. It started out by being a boatman's dream but ended up like a dopehead's nightmare,
and pardner, I reckon I should know.

This canal was the first one finished (or rather, I
should say opened) in Governor Broward's ambitious
scheme to "Drain the Everglades". The governor himself
was on hand to dig the first dipperful of earth in Ft.
Lauderdale's New River on July 4th, 1906. Eventually
this canal reached sixty-one miles through the Everglades to South Bay on the lake. Along its bank at the
present time is that heavily travelled road, part of U.S.
27, known officially as "Thomas E. Will Memorial Highway", in honor of the man whose unceasing efforts caused that highway to be built.

This water highway was the North New River, or
Lauderdale Canal. Of course there was a South New
River Canal as well. It ran west to the Miami Canal, but
except for a little early boating up to Davie, six miles or

eight from Ft. Lauderdale, it wasn't used for transportation.

The North Canal was dug from both ends, and when the dam was taken out on April 26, 1912, they held a celebration in Ft. Lauderdale when Albert W. Gilchrist, who was governor then, emptied a bottle of water from the Gulf of Mexico into New River. The governor's bottled water had hardly reached the sea before lake boats started using this shorter route to town. Besides the catfish boats there were all those passenger boats bringing land seekers and tourists, which now began making cross-state trips between Ft. Lauderdale and Ft. Myers. Menge's steamer SUWANEE, Forbes' MINDINAO, Moore's WANDERLUST and the LaROCHELLE from Palm Beach all were making regular trips. Even Andrew Mellon's big yacht VAGABONDIA came through, for there was plenty of water then. The lake was at its highest stage and water poured in a torrent between the staight black banks.

In the North Canal, six miles from town, the lake bound boat was lifted four or five feet in the locks.

LA ROCHELLE in the Locks, 1914.

OSCEOLA among the hyacinths of the Kissimmee River.   85

After that there was nothing much to look at all the remainder of the day excepting only for sawgrass as far as you could see, that is, unless you were of a mind to read the mileposts or look for alligators. Holloway's Canal branched off seven miles from town and returned four miles futher up. It enclosed the Plantation Tract, now one of Lauderdale's swankey subdivisions. On the left bank, the "Ten Mile Tree" provided a welcome shade in which the weary fisherman might tie his runboat while he slept off last night's jag, and the Fourteen Mile Hammock seemed oddly out of place in the midst of all that grassy water. Near the Fifteen Mile Post no banks rose on either side and here, during flood times, the southward flowing "Gulf Stream of the Everglades" swept across the canal's current, throwing the biggest boats off course. At Twenty Mile Post the canal's direction changed from nearly west to almost north for a six mile stretch.

Yacht VAGABONDIA of Andrew Mellon, passing Okeelanta
during the winter of 1913-14.

At this second bend where the dam had been, were the big wooden tanks which stored fuel for the dredges. It also was the end of the dredge men's telephone line of galvanized wire strung on two by fours. At 30½ miles, half way between the lake and coast, were laid up the dredge EVERGLADES and the sea going barge FERGUSON, once used as a reservoir for fuel oil. The only other landmarks to be seen in the long day's run were a discarded dredgeboat dipper, a broken boom, tangled lengths of cable, and as long as they lasted, the grave marker of DeSoto Tiger, killed by John Ashley the outlaw, and a land company's billboard sign. There was nothing else but sawgrass, as long and as far as you could look, until you reached the custard apples at the lake.

When this canal was being dug they had merely stripped the muck off down to the flat underlying limestone base, and that would have been fine if the water level had stayed high, but midway of its length that rock came nearer to the surface. When the lake went down,

Dam at 26 Mile Bend 1911. Barges and tow boat SECURITY of the Furst-Clark Construction Company.

then boats needed wheels to get over those miles of shoals. In 1916 the state had built locks at the lake end of each canal to hold back water in the lake, which only made things worse in the canals. So then the state got busy and dredged out a four mile channel half the width of the canal between mileposts 34 and 38 and built a wooden Temporary Lock and Spillway at milepost 36 and also at Twenty Mile Bend. For a while this eased the boatman's pain but the plagued lake still kept on going down. When aproaching the upper temporary locks a boat up-bound hugged the right hand bank, then, with no mark to show you where to turn, you'd make the Crossover to get into the dredged Half Channel. You had better look sharp to your steering here too, Bud, for that was where the LIBERTY I came to grief. Then a few miles above the Upper Temporary Lock business would start to picking up. For six, eight or ten miles according to the stage of water, you would start to pounding bottom if you didn't get stopped altogether.

Let me tell you what those shoals were like. It was while living at Okeelanta I had broken a tooth which was giving me most bodacious agony, so I decided to hop the first boat bound for town. There weren't but few boats running then for the canal was right smart low, but at first dark here came a fish runboat which I flagged down. It was the ALICE with Captain Wash Cross himself in his vest and gold watch chain. Inside the cabin was his boy "Cricket" at the wheel, while a young fisherman with flaming red hair was headed for his spree in town. Cap Cross allowed as how I could ride with him for $2, although if he'd said $5 I wouldn't have missed the trip, the way that tooth was jumping.

We were making good time down the canal in the pitchy darkness, until, after a couple of hours, Cap Cross called down to Cricket, "We'd ought to be a-seeing that butthead soon." A little later Cricket hollered back, "Aint you seen that blamed butthead yet?", then in fif-

teen minutes or so Cap shouted down "There's your butthead up ahead!" And there it was, an empty square ended skiff tied to the bank, though why it had been left
there I never knew However, it was the signal for
Cricket to slow his throttle a few notches, and not a mite
too soon, for the bow dipped as we felt the boat scrape
bottom. So now we'd reached the shoals!

Sometimes we'd grind and bump along, just barely
moving, sometimes we'd stop dead still. Then Cap Cross,
gold watch and all, the red headed fisherman and I
would all hop overboard. With our backs against the
boat's square transom and our hands clutching its bottom, we'd heave and raise, walking backward till the
boat could float again. The canal's bottom was smooth
rock, clean and almost level. It wasn't bad walking unless your foot bumped a loose boulder. Then you'd have
to dive under, pick it up and carry the blooming rock
to the bank. We'd slowed down a couple of dozen times
and got overboard half as many, when Cricket, sensing
that the worst was over, speeded up the engine. This
was mighty fine till Ka-rash!, with a jolt and a clatter
the runboat halted dead. From their rack above the
engine all the dry batteries and the ignition coil fell down
in a jumble of wires. The lantern tumbled to the floor
and promptly set fire to oil and gasoline in the bilge.
Cricket backed to the door, grabbed the extinguisher
and pumped like mad. Naturally, of course, the blamed
thing was empty. The cabin meanwhile was filled with
flames. It sure looked as if the runboat was a goner. A
heck of a place, I thought, to be stranded here half way
from nowhere, and with a blamed poor chance for another boat to be along before tomorrow or the next day.
But Redhead saved the day. Reaching through the open
window he grabbed a blanket from the bunk, soused it
overboard and tossed it back inside. Cricket then, by
dint of shouts and grunts and expletives, finally managed to smother out the flames. Then he re-lit the lantern,

searched around to find his batteries and coil, and tried
to get them all wired together properly once more. Cricket was cussing the rocks and the fire. Cap was cussing
Cricket for speeding up too soon. The redhead and I,
outside, were swatting right and left and cussing mosquitoes which had now discovered us. It was no small
commotion for awhile, till Cricket got his engine to popping. We scrambled overboard for the last time, got the
boat a-loose and finally made it to the Temporary Locks.

From there I knew we'd have no trouble, so as a
paying passenger, I made free to wring out the blanket
and roll up on the cabin roof, keeping my head well
covered from the skeeters. I'd slept an hour or two and
had plumb forgot my toothache, when Redhead woke
me from my snooze. "Reckon hit's about my turn for that
blanket now!", and so I let him have it.

The sun was lighting up the wooded shores when at
last we reached the river and in town I was the tooth
dentist's first customer that day.

My old daddy, who was always agitating to get the
canal improved, once wrote that navigating this canal
was " a combination of heroism and tragedy, including
wrecks without number, and beating and battering of
keels and propellers on rocks that were never blasted
out of the canal and boulders that lay loose in the bottom." Wrecks there were aplenty, but not too many sinkings. It takes water to sink a boat. Yet he was in one of
those sinkings himself, and that in deep water, too. It
seems that he was rather famous for coming clear from
narrow escapes, such as when a tornado wrecked the
White Belt Dairy at Hialeah and just missed the car he
was riding in. And another time, coming from Miami in
a crowded bus, he gave up his seat to a lady, which he
never failed to do. A couple of miles further as the bus
crossed the tracks at Hollywood, a locomotive plowed
right into that bus. It killed the lady who had taken his
seat but he didn't get a scratch.

This sinking happened on May 18, 1917. Dad had left Ft. Lauderdale in Aunapu's covered barge which was towed by the launch SYLVIA, also called N. B. BROWARD III. They had passed through the lower locks at first dark, where he had noticed that the spillway was holding back a right smart good head of water. Instead of sleeping below on the freight as usual, he had decided to bivouac on the roof. After winding his big gold watch, he placed it in his leather suitcase and strapped the lid down tight. Being an experienced traveller who believed in comfort, he had a couple of blankets rolled up and strapped, but before he could get the roll undone, the barge, with a terrific shock and shudder, struck something solid and promptly went down out of sight. Now, my father was no swimmer, but he had a death grip on that blanket roll, and as the bundles of paper tomato wraps came popping up, he grabbed one with the other hand and kept afloat until the launch came back and picked him up. That suitcase, though, he hated to lose, it had some valuable deeds and contracts as well as his clothes and watch. A few days later it was found by a state survey crew, and of all places, right in the edge of the Whirlpool, below the locks and miles from where the barge had sunk. But Dad's good luck was with him yet. His clothes, watch and papers were wet but not ruined, and he hadn't lost a thing, so I guess that goes to show you that it pays to live right. And that was when he learned about sinkings at first hand.

CHAPTER NINE

The Redoubtable Felix A. Forbes

When the land companies were putting on their high pressure sales campaigns, one of the first to be bitten by the Everglades bug was a Washington policeman, Felix A. Forbes, and a fine figure of a man he was, directing traffic at the Government Printing Office intersection. Tall, dark and handsome, that was Felix, in his snappy blue uniform and impressive black moustache. No wonder so many office girls found it convenient to cross at North Capitol and H.

With the opening of the settlement of Davie, six miles from Ft. Lauderdale, Felix threw up his job and took off for Florida. Davie (they called it Zona then, since so many of its settlers had just come from the Panama Canal Zone), was in the edge of the Everglades and was plagued with floods, but Forbes, with a beginner's luck, made a killing on some Irish potatoes. He bought the open, powered barge EVERGLADER and started hauling produce to town. Then he got ambitious and began the first scheduled cross state passenger runs from Ft. Lauderdale to Ft. Myers, with his glass cabin boats MAYFLOWER and DIXIE. It was a full day's run from either town to Ritta on the lake, where passengers would spend the night and continue on the following day. He had even started these runs before the dam had been remov-

ed from the canal. After getting the contract to carry
mail to Ritta, he put on an additional boat, a former
yacht, the MINDINAO, and a right peart looking boat
she was, with her clipper bow and bowsprit, her two
masts, a skiff boat hung from davits, and seats under a
canopy above her big glassed-in cabin. So many land
seekers and investors were using her for the cross state
trip that Forbes even built his own two story hotel on
the south end of Ritta Island.

MINDINAO of Forbes' Pioneer Boat Line. She was finally abandoned
near Forbes' hotel on Ritta Island, and her four cylinder Standard
engine was installed in the tug LEVIATHAN.

Business got so good that Felix sent out west for his two brothers. Jack, a hard bitten product of the deserts, farmed on the island, and after the government had got around to installing them, he tended beacon lights on the lake. Felix's other brother Edwin E., and Felix's son, Ed. Jr. ran the boats. It was a blamed good thing that he had got some help before he had his wreck, which happened one afternoon in the spring of 1915 as the DIXIE was proceeding peacefully up the canal. Felix was sorting out the mail for Okeelanta, when with a sickening jolt, the boat hit a piece of discarded dredgeboat iron and she began to fill. The passengers all got ashore on the weed grown bank, but it was hours later before a passing runboat picked them up and carried them on to Ritta. Meanwhile, Felix had dived time after time inside the boat, although only part of her top was above the water. He saved the mail and some of the passengers valuables, but the film of gasoline on top of the water filled his nose and ears with blistering effect.

Forbes' DIXIE which Sunk in the Canal.

Next day Forbes came back from Ritta with blocks and tackles and long timbers on a barge. At Okeelanta he picked up half a dozen settlers and the captain of the dredge then digging the Bolles Canal. By the time we had got to where the DIXIE lay, fifteen miles from the lake, the gasoline in his nose and ears had taken effect so that he acted like anything but the foreman for a salvage crew. Between prodgious feats of swimming, diving and aimless splashing around he took frequent swigs from the dredgeman's bottle, in which the latter joined with gusto. As a consequence, no great sight was accomplished except confusion, until they both took off for town in the dredge's launch. The farmers then went to work and partly raised the boat so that a crew from town with more equipment could finish up the job.

After a good many weeks and several hospital operations, Capt. Forbes resumed his piloting, his right ear a shapeless cauliflower from which a quill projected. It was after this that folks remarked on how Capt. Forbes didn't seem to be his former hearty, jolly self. He got irritable at nothing, and sometimes pulled some right strange pranks, such as one that Dick LeFils used to tell about.

It seems that on one of his trips from Lauderdale the captain had as a passenger a saleman bound for Little Bare Beach. Now, for some reason unknown to us, this salesman had rubbed the good skipper the wrong way. Capt. Forbes was irked, he was pleasured not at all. All the way up that monotonous canal he chewed his mustache and sulled and brooded all day long. Next morning the MAYFLOWER left the hotel at Ritta in what was the third day of a heck of a northwest blow. As they neared the long Bare Beach dock, Forbes called the salesman over to him.

"You can plainly see that it's too rough for me to tie up to the dock. Now, I'm going to run dead slow past the end of it and when I swing the stern in, all you've got to do is step off between those two tall pilings. The dock is under water but you won't mind getting your feet wet I suppose!"

Mr. Salesman rolled up his pants, hung his shoes around his neck, and with his grip in hand, confidently stepped off between the pilings. Dick says that as the boat, with full throttle, headed for the open lake, the last seen of the salesman he was spouting water like a porpoise as he shinned up one of those stobs. Dick thinks that Cap must have forgot to tell the man that the storm had washed the dock away.

CHAPTER TEN

The Invincible "Palm"

If you had been around the lake in the old boating days you couldn't help but know the old "Palm". More than likely you rode in her now and again. The old boat could change her appearance oftener than a Bimini rum runner, but she was tough as old whang leather, for she survived four years of beating her bottom in the Lauderdale canal and escaped destruction in a couple of hurricanes and once saved Arthur Fitzhugh from losing $16,000, but I will maybe get around to that a little later.

Captain Norman Richard Fitzhugh had lived in the ancient village of Picolata on the St. Johns just west of St. Augustine, where he had hauled oranges on the river since the memory of man runneth not to the contrary. In the year of 1916 his boat was a 34 foot skipjack with a hiked up bow and stern, a sharp V bottom and a windowless cabin. But Model T trucks had ruined the orange business so the good skipper was looking for greener waters when he learned that bids were called for to haul mail from Ft. Lauderdale to Ritta. If'n the old captain had made just one trip up that canal with a sounding rod, he might have said "To heck with the U. S. Mail. I'll sell my boat and buy a farm!" But with the blythe optomism of blissful ignorance he underbid Forbes, and then discovered that he acquired a very white and a powerful hungry elephant. Now, his skipjack might have been a blamed good boat in the St. Johns River, but Lake Okeechobee had dropped from better than 20 feet elevation to 17. The PALM drew 38 inches light and in the canal 38 inches was considered to be pretty tolerably deep soundings. So about the first thing Fitzhugh had to do was to cut some of that V off her bottom and add nine feet to her kicked-up stern. That didn't help a heap, for the canal kept getting shoaler, so he made her bottom completely flat and added fifteen more feet to her length. She was supposed to carry passengers, but for a long time the accommodations were boxes of freight

Fitzhugh's PALM entering Locks at Canal Point. Custard Apple Inn in Background.

in the windowless cabin, where in bad weather with the side doors closed, all you could do was sprawl around and wonder how much longer it was going to be. In that long stretch above the Temporary Lock she would bump and grind and wallow along. When she stopped altogether the passengers would wade ashore and heave and pull on the rope until she floated again. It got so that, believe it or not, there was a right good towpath along that canal bank.

Her schedule called for leaving Ft. Lauderdale at 7:30 A.M. When water had been better, Forbes had used to reach Okeelanta, 57 miles up, about 5 o'clock in the afternoon, then Ritta, fifteen miles further, about 7:00 or 8:00. But the poor old PALM would get to Okeelanta anytime between ten and midnight, even later sometimes. On mail nights the settlers at Okeelanta and South Bay used to congregate, do their little trading in the stores, then swap gossip and wait. By ten or eleven, if they didn't see the PALM'S light down the canal, they would crank up their launches and pop-pop home.

The captain hadn't been long on the run when he was joined by his son Arthur. They usually were the whole crew. Every Sunday the poor old PALM would be hauled out on the ways. At church Mrs. Fitzhugh's greetings to her friends invariably was, "Well, the boat's on the ways again, and this time the Captain says it's a broken propeller" (or maybe a bent shaft, a twisted rudder, a leaking garboard seam or a sprung butt joint, according to the circumstances). It got so that the Fitzhughs finally devised an ingenious scheme to save both time and money. They carried a spare propeller wheel mounted on a shaft, and put a permanent guide wire from the boat's bottom down to the skeg, or shoe. Now when a blade got bent or broken off a man stepped into the boat which they always towed, slipped a rope over the wheel and pulled the shaft clear out of its stuffing boxes. Then, aided by the guide wire, the spare shaft with it propeller was neatly slipped into place. They got so good that they could change shafts in 30 minutes, to the amazement of their passengers, one of whom once exclaimed " I have traveled by boat from Canada to Key West but that's the first time I ever saw a propeller installed in a floating boat without somebody getting wet!"

The canal was a headache but the lake could be bad too, but in a different way. Like I was saying, it takes water to sink a boat, but Arthur managed to sink the PALM in water only four feet deep. One night a squall caught him somewhere between Kreamer and Ritta Islands. Arthur was the only one aboard except his brother-in-law, who had never before been in a boat. All the boat's side and deck seams had opened up from sun and drought and the water poured inside faster that it could be pumped out. Finally the engine conked out and she swung broadside and filled and sunk. Arthur sure had a time trying to run on schedule.

The PALM was as much a freighter as a passenger boat and so during the war, when you couldn't hire even sorry help, Arthur and the old captain were the crew. Handling all those crates and hampers, grocery boxes and drums of gasoline, besides steering and locking the boat through four different locks, was no kind of a job for grey hairs. The captain was the first one to come down sick, but he had hardly got back before Arthur was laid up. Then it seemed like the skipper's stooped figure took on an additional droop when the post office department, yielding to the settlers' importunities, decreed in 1919 that the PALM must run three round trips a week. Now the men were home only on Sundays and most likely making repairs even then. Arthur's children hardly knew their daddy's face.

As if bumping bottom in the canal wasn't bad enough, they had their troubles in handling mail sacks and cargo at Ritta. The PALM might have to anchor a quarter mile offshore and ferry passengers and freight by rowboat. They finally got a seinboat rigged with an airplane engine and propeller which helped a heap. This was the first airplane engine most lake people had ever seen. On night runs, mullet jumping into the boat kept them well supplied with fish.

But the immediate reason why they bought the seinboat was because of what happened once at Ritta. A farmer there wanted to ship 54 hampers of potatoes, but Fitzhugh said "no dice". The PALM lay 100 yards away hard and fast aground and besides he knew that already in South Bay and Okeelanta there was more than a full load waiting him. But the farmer paid Miss Maud Wingfield to stamp his hampers and ship them by parcel post, so the captain and Arthur had to shirt tail all 54 of them out to the PALM, which took so long that the return trip to town consumed 25 hours. The heck of it was that instead of collecting his customary 25c per hundred pounds, the potatoes, being U. S. mail, had to be hauled for nothing.

Meanwhile Fitzhugh had changed his boat again. This time he lengthened her out to a full 64 ft .11 inches, the longest she could be without being documented. This reduced her draft to only 30 inches, and that was still too much. But he also had to put in a bigger engine. After purchasing a new six cylinder 120 horsepower Peerless to replace the 25 horse four cylinder of the same make, he didn't have the money to pay for its installation.

Consequently, between their arrival one Saturday night and departure Monday morning, Norman, Arthur and the deckhand removed the old engine, built a new engine bed, set in and aligned the engine and then installed new fuel, water and exhaust pipes and left for the lake about as much on time as usual.

Demand for transportation in the post-war years increased until Capt. Fitzhugh conceived the ambitious plan of building another and shallower draft boat. The result was the SAGO, sixty-four feet eleven inches by eighteen feet beam, with cargo space below and seats under a canopy on the upper deck and a pilot house forward. There were two mis-matched engines, a Vulcan and a Fairbanks Morse, whose propellers turned in tunnels. The SAGO was big and impressive looking but what with mechanical troubles and first one thing and another, she was just another elephant of a different color, so Fitzhugh finally unloaded her on the Clewiston Development Company where she eventually sunk in their Industrial Canal.

The canal settlers didn't like it, but the Fitzhughs must have whooped with joy when the post office department changed the mail run from Ft. Lauderdale to West Palm Beach. The PALM now docked in the Palm

Fitzhugh's SAGO, "An elephant of a different color."

Beach Canal between West Palm Beach and Lake Worth. She stopped at postoffices in Loxahatchee and Canal Point then across the lake at Ritta, Bare Beach and Moore Haven, but not at Clewiston. Heck, there wasn't any Clewiston. Sub-contractors carried mail to Pahokee, Bacom Point, Keamer, Tory, Chosen, Belle Glade, South Bay and Okeelanta.

After a good road had been built from West Palm Beach to Loxahatchee Dairy, thus lopping sixteen miles from the water route, Fitzhugh invested in a bus to carry his passengers this far, and after completion of Conners Highway, to haul them right on to Canal Point. Fitzhugh didn't have the first bus in the Everglades, for the McCoys were already using one, a station wagon, but he had the first enclosed bus and it really was a dilly. It had been built in a buggy factory in Jacksonville for a reputed sum of $12,500, was a square as a house and those clumsy wooden window frames would rattle on that rough rock road till it sounded like the battle of Gettysburg. The driver was no less than DeWitt Upthegrove, later to be county supervisor of registration. Still, it seemed to be a darned good bus, considering.

But early in 1922 after the railroad was extended, a post office was established in Clewiston. Since it was now the most centrally located railhead, all lake mail was shipped from this town and the Fitzhughs lost the mail contract. However, the Clewiston Development Company now hired the PALM for 12 months at $150 per month, to carry land prospects from West Palm Beach to this new metropolis of the lake.

It was at this time that Barron G. Collier's Tamiami Trail Tours was getting started. It already was running busses and trucks from Tampa to Everglades City but wanted to branch eastward too. Their plan was to run a bus from Ft. Myers to Moore Haven and a boat across the lake, so Arthur Fitzhugh, who now was managing the business, agreed that for $16,000 he'd sell them his bus and his PALM boat too. Arthur already owed the Moore Haven bank a whopping $10,000 and had an ample number of other debts besides, but the blasted T.T.T. seemed to be in no hurry to pay off.

At last the check arrived. Arthur could hardly sleep that night. Next morning you may be sure, the first customer in the Moore Haven bank was Mr. Arthur Fitzhugh, somewhat fidgety lest payment already had been stopped. It was September 17, 1926. In the Western Union window a telegram proclaimed that Miami was being destroyed. Arthur cashed his check, paid his note and got away from there right fast. The following morning there no longer was a Western Union office nor a bank. The huricane had eliminated Moore Haven too. Howsomever, the old PALM escaped and went right on running across the lake.

Arthur took what little he had left after paying all his debts, and opened a news stand and bookie joint in Lake Worth. He'd had a plumb sufficiency of boating.

CHAPTER ELEVEN

Last Boat to Lauderdale

Although Forbes and Fitzhugh carried passengers from Lauderdale longer than any other boatmen, those were the days of free enterprise and anybody could start a transportation line who had the money and the urge, so other boats were carrying passengers to the lake as well. One was the LAKEPORT which ran to the town

LAKEPORT at Okeechobee City 1915.

ALLURE in Ft. Lauderdale, 1919. "A Beauty of a Boat,
all Mahogany and Brass."

of that name when it was starting up, but the captain
died while on the lake, and his young son, the only other
person on board, had to bring the boat on down to Ft.
Lauderdale, and that was the last trip of the LAKE-

Wrecking the ALLURE in 1926. "It Seemed a Sacrilegious
Thing to Do."

QUEEN OF THE GLADES in Lower Locks. Enthusiastic Land
Seekers Headed for Lake Okeechobee.

Warren's SKYLARK, a land company boat, at Belle Glade.

PORT. Then there was the ALLURE which ran to Okeechobee City, a beauty of a boat to be sure, a former
yacht, with gleaming, long, white hull and a cabin all
mahogany and brass. Her captain, Swanson, had attached the boat for wages due him and put her on the lake
run to make her earn her keep. Her principal stop was
at Okeelanta which was booming then, to which the
round trip fare was only $5 and where meals and rooms
in the hotel could be had for 35 and 50 cents. But it
seemed that few people wanted to go on to Okeechobee
City, so after several changes of ownership, all for the
worse, the ALLURE was brought to the boat yard which
I was operating at the time, to be broken up for junk,
which, having known her in her glory, seemed a sacrilegious thing to do.

The land selling companies ran boats of their own,
for they couldn't afford to have their trusting prospects
contaminated by "knockers" who had already come here
and learned the score. R. J. Bolles, the first and biggest
of the "sawgrass merchants" owned the large glass
cabin boat QUEEN OF THE GLADES. Capt. Charlie
Murray, former skipper of the steamer SUWANEE, ran
her first from Ft. Myers, and then from Ft. Lauderdale,
up to Ritta as long as the Bolles Hotel was operating.
Bryant & Greenwood used the DIXIE QUEEN, Warren
the SKYLARK, H. H. Hart the MACUSHLA, and James
A. Moore the open O U VIM, fastest of them all. These
boats all came up from Lauderdale, but the very last
boat to carry passengers on that canal was the PASSING
THRU, which I ran on her last scheduled trip December
24, 1921, and a heck of a trip it was, I'll have you know.
PASSING THRU was a glass cabin boat, beamy and of
shallow draft. Clint Stone, her owner, had started out by
hauling freight from the settlements on Hillsboro Canal
in 1918, but the next winter he carried only passengers,
though in a covered seinboat pushed ahead, he might
haul a few hampers of produce or a rare negro laborer.

The following fall, since I had been away from the lake and he knew a few things which I did not, Clint persuaded me that the way to get prosperous was to take over his passenger run. There were no other passenger boats on the canal, and that should have been a warning, for changes were taking place. The state, apparently determined to discourage settlement in the Glades, was doing not a thing to encourage navigation. The canal was low and getting clogged with hyacinths. Instead of collecting toll on the boat and passengers at only one lock as before, the state now had started collecting almost as much at locks on each end of each canal, and we had to pass through three. Then by this time, there were other ways to get to town. A canal bank, not yet leveled off, had been thrown up from Loxahatchee to Belle Glade, with pontoons for bridges at each of the canal crossings. So now it was possible, if you had a worm drive truck, a couple of helpers and some pry poles, to get to the coast and back in a single day, whereas before it had been a three day trip to get to the county seat and back. Then too, if you had some way to get to Canal Point, boats left

PASSING THRU at Okeelanta in 1919. L E. Will's Home at Left. J. M. Baker's Store at Right. Clinton Stone, owner, with his son Eddie on deck.

there most every day for West Palm Beach.

All that fall the PASSING THRU made two weekly round trips to Belle Glade and didn't make expenses, but at last came Christmas Eve day and it looked like the whole Everglades wanted to go to town. As usual the trip began at Capt. Wurtz's farm two miles east of Belle Glade, the last houses down the canal if you didn't count abandoned Glade Crest. Cranking up in the morning darkness at 5:30 A.M., I stopped at Myer's Hotel and all the other landings, picking up passengers and crates and hampers along the way. Since the farmers had a most unpleasant habit of dumping moonvines, old overalls and shirts into the canal, you'd have to get overboard while stopped at "Stein's Locks" in Chosen, dive

Meyer Hotel in Belle Glade, 1921. First stop for the PASSING THRU on her way to Ft. Lauderdale.

under her bottom in that chilly water with a sharp knife and whack and saw the cussed garbage from the propeller while the sun struggled to break through the clouds. The run to Torry was not too bad, but from there to South Bay the former lake bottom squatters had also used the canal for a dumping ground, with now and again a wire fish trap to make life more interesting. Okeelanta would be the principal stop on the trip. Here I'd get overboard for the last time to clear the wheel. Then all too soon I had to slow down for the shoals. By moving the crates and passengers forward, I did right well without knocking her bottom out, but then the goldinged engine tried to quit. It was located in the stern while the gas tank was in the bow, the gasoline was getting low and it wouldn't flow up hill. Disconnecting and blowing out the gas line did no good, so the deckhand had to feed gasoline into the carburetor with a coffee can till we got down to the Half Channel. The engine didn't seem to approve of this too much and went to coughing, spitting and sputtering like a bull calf with the croup. It's a thousand wonders we didn't catch afire there in the exact middle of nowhere, and with no other boats likely to come along for a day or two, but with this and that, we kept chugging along and finally tied up in Ft. Lauderdale at the foot of Brickell Avenue. It was 3:30 Christmas morning. I toted some of the lady passenger's goway bags to the hotel, and I reckon that was about the last time I've walked barefooted up the main street of Ft. Lauderdale—well the last time on a Christmas day, at any rate.

There wasn't ary a single crying passenger showed up for the return trip to the lake, which suited me very well. I hunted up Clint Stone, told him he could have his boat, and went and got myself a job fighting mosquitoes on a dredge boat at Cape Sable. And that there trip was the last time ary a passenger boat ran between Lauderdale and the lake.

CHAPTER TWELVE

Big Foot Bill, The Swede

It may seem right strange that for so many years people by the hundreds, even thousands, had been travelling to Lake Okeechobee, and yet it wasn't till World War One that any freight boats were running on the lake. Except for catfish and their ice, there was nothing much to bring in nor haul out. The nation wide land selling campaign had brought prospective settlers by the jillions to "see the Everglades", but heck, they couldn't even find the land they'd bought, much less make a living on it. Some few did stay a while in the "sawgrass settlements" which sprung up overnight, then died like Jonah's gourd. Then those people either went back home or squatted on the lake. After the Big Freeze in 1917 a heap more folks from everywhere came to the lakeshore too, where warm land could be had just for the clearing of it. All these settlers had to have supplies, and if they were lucky, they'd have some tomatoes and peppers to ship, and that was when freight boats started running to the lake, for the mailboats couldn't tote it all. As long as that canal could be navigated, most all traffic went to Ft. Lauderdale, even though there were railroads in Okeechobe and Moore Haven, and even after the canal was opened to West Palm Beach. Although a good many freight boats ran to Lauderdale, the main skippers were John Ziegler, John Annapu and Big Foot Bill.

One of the first to try running freight on this canal
had been John Ziegler in 1917. His boat, the LIBERTY,
was a cypress hulled, square bowed sternwheeler built
at Davie by John Aunapu, but before he'd made many
trips Ziegler ripped her bottom out at the Cross Over
up the canal. Then he built the LIBERTY II, of two inch
pine, 18 feet beam and just under 65 feet in length. She
had a canopy and pilot house above and a housed-in lower deck, and the engine and paddlewheel from the original boat. This engine, the first and maybe the only
Diesel engine in any freighter on the lake, was a 15
horsepower horizontal, single cylinder Fairbanks Morse,
a "hot head", which meant that you had to light a blow-
torch, and heat a metal plug in the cylinder head when
ever you had to crank it up. The engine was so hard to
start and fuel was so cheap that the engine almost never
was shut down. The LIBERTY might be tied up all day
long, but that "pow-pow-pow" of her unmuffled exhaust
would wake the echos of the custard apple swamps,
while the whole boat shook and vibrated till it was a

Heaney's PEGGY at South Bay. "With His Family for a Crew and
a Hatful of Kerosene for Fuel, She didn't Cost Much to Run."

thousand wonders that she could hold together. But hold together she did, and, until all but Big Foot Bill had abandoned the canal, she kept on pow-powing down to Lauderdale. During the last year or two the hyacinths like to have got Ziegler stopped, but he was an ingenious cuss. He rigged a chopper to cut a channel through. This was a two bladed propeller out in front, on a shaft through the stem post, run by a Kermath engine, and it chopped right through those weeds, but at last they got too bad even for Johnny Ziegler, so he sold his boat and got himself a filling station in town.

Most boats, by this time, were gasoline engine, propeller boats, but there was one other sternwheeler which ran here too, and that was Heaney's PEGGY. Boatmen didn't carry their wives along, but Heaney went to extremes, he carried his whole family, his wife, two boys and a girl. They all had once lived in a houseboat at Okeelanta until Heaney decided to go to hauling freight. He lengthened his houseboat not once but twice and added a pilot house. His paddlewheel was driven by a one cylinder stationary Witte engine which ran on kerosene. There was no reverse gear, so he had to drift to make a stop and that called for some fancy footwork by his deckhand when he made a landing down stream with the wind behind. With his family for a crew and a hatful of kerosene for fuel, it didn't cost Heaney much to run, but that PEGGY boat was slow, good grief, but was she slow! On one trip, and with a paying passenger, too, he was eight days from Ft. Lauderdale to Chosen! If Heaney hadn't carried his family along he never would have got to see them.

Of all the ill favored boats which ran the canal there was none so ugly as the freighter NEW OKEELANTA. After returning from the war I ran this misbegotten craft for near onto a year from the lake to Lauderdale, and during summer months, clear on to Miami. Brand new, she had been built for Ludwig Franz, Okeelanta's lumber man, by a house carpenter in Okeechobee, whose chief tools, it seemed, must have been a plumb bob and a square. Her house (of lapped siding of all things) was square as any box, while perched on her upper deck a fugitive country toilet served as a pilot house. And then, to cap it all, she was both slow and clumsy. But there's always some good in the ugliest of us, and NEW OKEE-LANTA could run in shallow water. Her cypress hull and house gave her light weight, and a universal joint in the propeller shaft allowed the wheel to be raised up. However, that house carpenter had hung her rudder so high that it wasn't in the slip stream of the propeller, so she didn't steer at all. So then, instead of rigging it so it could be lowered, he just added two more rudders, which like the first were still too high. Although Franz was a whiz at figuring profits, he couldn't understand that an efficiency of three times nothing would still result in zero, so he wouldn't have it changed.

Franz had searched Miami's junkyards, and returned with a three cylinder engine, a Pearl, possibly the only one of its kind (I hope). The caps of its connecting rods

The Author on NEW OKEELANTA. "There's Some Good in the Ugliest of Us", Okeelanta 1919.

were held by a hinge on one side and single bolt on the other, and how those blamed caps could vibate loose! And the compression was so weak that I could change spark plugs without stopping the engine. This was a routine chore, but there were plenty of others. Keeping that Pearl engine going was an education.

The crew consisted of Ludwig's son Frank and myself. Frank did his share of handling heavy work, but mostly he was deckhand and supercargo. In town he could perform prodigies of trading and trafficking, but on the boat he'd never touch the engine (if he did, I'd wish he hadn't), nor would he trust himself to make a landing, enter a lock, nor even pass a big boat in the canal. The blamed old boat was so cussed slow that we never tied up to rest except when in town, so between messing with that engine and doing most all the steering, I got three or four hours sleep on the two day trip, and was always short a night or two by the end of the week. A pot of black coffee is the steerman's friend, but did you ever try holding your eyes open with your fingers? Of course, a bump against the muck bank of the canal would have done no harm, but there was always the chance of meeting some zig-zagging fishboat whose pilot also might be suffering from shut-eye, of if up bound, more likely from redeye.

Still, freight boating could have its bright moments too. During the summer months we ran to Miami, which then was a good sized town. There were two theaters there, so we always tried to get tied up at Lyons Wharf at the foot of Flagler Street in time to walk to the Airdrome down by the bay. We would see the vaudeville show there, then skipping the motion picture, we'd hurry to the other theater to see the live performance there. Then, next day on the way back home, reflecting on the songs, the comedians' antics and the pretty girls, helped relieve the monotony of that long, slow drag up the canal.

One night, half way through the show, somebody must have opened up a quart of Scotch. The actors muffed their lines, the comedians got fouled up and started pulling last week's jokes, the chorus girls gyrated most unsteadily, while the vocalist had to hang onto the scenery to sing her solos. The young and shapely star in hip length black tights, her eyes shining like stars in the spotlight, undulated her delicious figure while she carolled joyously,

'You boys have seen my ruby lips but you want
to take notice of my wicked hips!''

The audience shouted and whistled, the performers laughed and waved back in delight. Everybody had a right enjoyable time, and I reckon that was near about the most successful performance of the whole ding busted summer.

If the NEW OKEELANTA was the ugliest, then the NEW RIVER must have been the finest freighter that ever ran the canal, though she didn't run there long.

NEW RIVER, 63.3' x 16.1' with 60 HP Jansic Automobile Type engine. Skippered by the author. Shown here at Dillevig's Boat Yard, Ft. Lauderdale. "She was a boatman's dream".

She had been built in 1920 by the boat builder S. Dillevig for himself, at the same time he was building Fitzhugh's SAGO. She was intended for the passenger trade, but she was built too late in the game. On her upper deck, instead of a canopy such as the SAGO had, was a big cabin with twenty bunks, hinged and curtained like a Pullman Car, and a dining saloon which could seat twenty people. Forward was a spacious pilot house with an inlaid steering wheel salvaged from some yacht. She even had electric lights! Her single screw turned in a half tunnel so she drew only 20 inches light and 28 or 30 with a load. She was a boatman's dream.

Her first job had been hauling sugarcane. The Pennsylvania Sugar Company had bought a large acreage 16 miles up the Miami Canal at Pennsuco, where Graham's Dairy is. They had scoured the country for seed cane, particularly for D74, of which the farmers on Lake Okeechobee's shores and islands had aplenty. NEW RIVER, along with other boats, hauled this cane down the canal to Lauderdale, through the Inland Waterway and Biscayne Bay, then up the Miami River and canal. This was at the same time that the first causeway was being built across Biscayne Bay. It was nearly finished except that the drawbridge hadn't been installed, although the high concrete abutments were completed, and they were a favorite place from which to fish. According to Dillevig's account of it, the NEW RIVER was returning empty up the bay and heading for the gap where the drawbridge was supposed to be. Capt. Shackleford noticed as he got closer that there seemed to be quite a passel of women out that day fishing from those piers. Some of them waved to him and his chest swelled with pride to think that he was skipper of so fine a craft. There was right smart of a breeze that afternoon. The bay was choppy and he couldn't scarcely see the channel for all those skirts a-flapping up there in the wind. So then, first news he knew, his boat was heading dead-on for that concrete

abutment and it was too cussed late to turn aside. He
rang every bell in the house for "Astern, Full Speed,"
but just as the engineer was backing up like mad, the
boat with a terrific crash, ran full tilt into that concrete
wall, so hard, in fact, that she actually bounced right
back. The engineer went sailing over his engine, taking
the reverse gear lever with him as he went, and slammed
the engine into full speed ahead again, and so she rammed
that wall once more. Well, after awhile I reckon the boat
gave up trying to knock that abutment down and she
somehow got back home. When Dillevig heard about it
he nearly blew a fuse until he found his boat wasn't hurt
too much, except for needing a new cutwater, not to men-
tion a new captain. Since she was documented with the
Steamboat Commission, he had to have a licensed master,
so that's how come I then hung my ticket in her pilot
house.

After I had made a few trips to the lake fetching
tomatoes from Bare Beach, but not a crying passenger,

Big Foot Bill's Launch and Barges Hauling Potatoes from Walter
Greer's Farm at Belle Glade to Ft. Lauderdale, 1918.

Dillevig decided the lake was not for her, and sold the boat to a concern in Miami which ripped off those beautiful upper works, changed her name, installed a glass in her bottom, and put her on sightseeing tours to the "Sunken Gardens" off Cape Florida.

These big double decked freight boats did very well when there was water in the canal, but the very last boat to make this run, as it also had been one of the first to start, was a barge pulled by a launch. It's owner was a famous Swede, Bill Wellen was his name. He was known far and wide as Big Foot Bill, though why, he couldn't say, ("My feet aind no bigger tan no vun else's".)

Bill had started back in '17 with his launch and open barge, picking up what little jags of vegetables he could find from Little Bare Beach to as far as Belle Glade, and hauling them down the Ft. Lauderdale Canal. Long after all other boats had quit, he battled the rocks and hyacinths. He had the canal all to himself. After that he moved to the Brown Farm down the Hillsboro and hauled to the railroad in Belle Glade.

Bill seldom carried any helper so he never ran at night. You could be running across the lake, about three-fourths asleep and there would be Bill's launch and barge snugged down at anchor under a riding light. I joked him about being the only freight boat man who never ran at night. "Ya, dot night vork iss no goot" he said, "Ay likes mine schleep. Ven effer a nap comes down, dere's vare Ay drops mine sphud hook!"

After Bill had been freighting for a few years he housed in his barge, built a little living room in one corner and carried his wife along for company. According to lake scuttlebut Bill had acquired this lady in an informal sort of shotgun wedding, but then women used to be powerful scarce and a man had to get one as best he could and not be too blamed choosy always about such things as looks. Anyway they seemed to get along right well together so long as Bill was in his launch and she stayed on the barge. But Bill had one little trait that really irked his wife. He liked to keep a jug of drinking liquor under his steering seat and during those long, slow drags down the canal he loved to take a sip now and again to sort of pass the time. If Mrs. Bill caught him at it she would surely bawl him out, and as a bawler-outer she was good. Bill was a patient sort of man but sometimes he'd get riled.

"Von time ven Ay vos dakting a schwig vrom te bottle she holler at me 'Bill! Bill!', but Ay don't pay her no mind. Ten she start pulling on te towline and schwing te boat around. Ay don't like tat much. Ay kvick sthop te engine and te olt lady she go head virst offerboart, sthill hanging to te towrope. Ay dunk her goot, too, bevore Ay pull her oud!"

Nevertheless, and in spite of all, they got along right well, and the good lady saved his money for him and bought a nice home in town against the day when they no longer could frolic on the lake.

CHAPTER THIRTEEN

John Aunapu, He Made His Negroes Happy

Everybody on the south shore knew John Aunapu, for he was the pioneer and kingpin of freighting on the canal. He started out with nothing but a smart idea and wound up with a fleet of boats, a farm, and money in the old sock besides. John had been born across the water in Estonia on the Gulf of Finland, but he denied that he was a "tamn Rooshian." After he had knocked around in merchant ships for seven or eight years, and had become skipper of the yacht of one of the owners of the Metropolitan Opera Company, John heard about the Everglades. He bought ten acres at eighty dollars each, from Vance W. Helm, threw up his job and went to farm in Davie. Conditions there were mighty new and raw but things looked promising, so he sent to the old country for his wife and young son Frede (which is pronounced Freddy by the way). The first winter they planted five acres of Irish potatoes which grew and thrived mightily just as the land company had said they would, but one week before time to dig, the water started coming up until it covered the ground. It still kept coming up until it covered the vines, which the land company had not said one word about. This was a terrible blow to John, but his wife was plumb heartbroken. She would have gone back to Courland but all their money was in the ground and it a foot under water. But John was pretty sharp. Since water had been his ruin it was going to be his salvation. He scrounged around, got hold of a barge, and a launch named SYLVIA and started hauling from Davie to Ft. Lauderdale. Then with the help of his friend Howard Stowe from Torry Island, and some borrowed money, he set about building the boat that was to make him famous. They built her right on the canal bank there at Davie, a 45 foot black hulled freighter with a half-tunnel stern and a 28 horse power Clifton, liberated from a junk yard, and he quite appropriately named her N. B. BROWARD.

After making a few trips to Lauderdale, John in January 1916 headed for greener waters on the lake. The BROWARD wasn't very large but was as big as any freight boat then on the lake, and she was the very first to try to run on a schedule. Settlers were scarce and John had to range pretty far afield to find anything to haul. He cruised from Lake Port and Moore Haven on the west, to East Beach on the other shore, but as settlers and their produce increased he reduced his run to Ritta, Belle Glade, South Bay and Okeelanta. Of course, other freight boats started cutting in, but John's devotion to his customer's interests, and his regular schedules, made him a favorite with the farmers and with the merchants too. He lengthened the BROWARD out to 60 feet, enclosed the lower deck and built benches and a canopy on top for passengers. With that tunnel stern she drew only two feet light, so she could haul a heavy load, besides, for a freight boat (or for any boat for that matter) she was pretty fast. John said she could make nine miles an hour when empty, but since she was never empty how in the dickens could he tell? Anyhow, she could make three round trips weekly and that wasn't bad.

John soon had so much business that he got an additional boat, the glass cabin HERMINE which had hauled material for contractor Young in building the canal locks. She had a two cylinder 25 horsepower Globe which swung a 32 inch propeller, and a reverse gear as big as flour barrel and generally out of order. The cylinders, which stood nearly as high as the engineer, were capped with a single head for both, and when I say it took two men to pick up that head, I don't just speak from hearsay. Later John acquired a launch with a 4 cylinder Speedway which he called N. B. BROWARD III, the HERMINE being number II.   The launch towed a covered barge, the same one which sunk with Dr. Will. So Johnny was now in the class with Capt. Clay Johnson and the Menges. He was a fleet owner.

John was mighty popular with the farmers and their wives too, for he did their shopping for them while in town. Of course, most boat captains spent considerable time delivering orders to the stores in town for anything from a spool of thread to a drum of gasoline or a jag of lumber for a house, but John was more reliable than the rest. He seldom forgot what he was supposed to get, and that is most remarkable for he never wrote down anything. Whereas other skippers carried a well worn notebook to record the orders and the prices he had paid, for merchants didn't credit those lake folks much, John kept every item in his head.

John wasn't much of a man for size, but he had the energy of two. John handled freight along with the crew and did most of the steering besides. Worst of all, he expected everybody else to keep up with him. Consequently, with three trips a week and all that freight to handle, sleep was a scarce commodity and the poor boys went around in a daze. I'll tell you what I mean. One night I was a passenger on the BROWARD. As she steamed up New River, I went below to survey the heaped up cargo and look for a flat place to lie down and sleep. The young engineer, a second generation Swede from Davie named Olaf Freitag, checked and oiled his engine, then plumb tuckered out, he stretched out on a wide plank, well polished by use, between the engine and the galley bulkhead, and instantly was fast asleep. As we approached the locks six miles up, John clanged the bell one "bong" to slow the engine. Ole heard it but that was all. He twisted, he groaned, he waved his hands but he couldn't come awake. Talk about somebody fighting sleep, it was no figure of speech! John had to bang that gong again before Ole came to life and slowed the engine. Another time Ole got his long blond hair into the magneto as he rolled around, with shocking results to himself, and a good bawling out when the BROWARD rammed the gates of the lock.

But Ole was not the only sleepyhead. Once Frede was decking for his father on the HERMINE as she towed a barge. At this same lower locks Frede jumped ashore still four-thirds asleep, to make the HERMINE fast. He walked the catwalk clear to the end and right off into ten feet of water. When they got to the locks at Twenty Mile Bend it was drizzling rain. Frede jumped to the lock wall, slipped and went sprawling into the canal again. Below the 36 mile locks John decided that Frede had had enough sleep for one night, stopped the boat and called him to come and steer. Frede crawled out of the barge, rubbing sleep from his eyes and stepped right into the gap between the barge and launch, and that made three baths inside of 30 miles.

When John started boating he still kept his place at Davie which was farmed by his wife and Frede, but before the first year was done, he moved them to the lake where he took possession of Bird and Loomis Islands of 76 and 40 acres respectively, which lay unclaimed and almost inaccessible among the hyacinths between Torry and the mainland. As the lake receded he farmed some surrounding lake bottom too. All of this land is now part of the Belle Glade Country Club, and pastures there abouts.

John cleared custard apples from the islands, and with a huge home made rake, raked off the moonvine mat which had grown over the lake bottom land. He also built himself a couple of mighty efficient tractors, and later on, a dredge. On this lake bottom he planted one three acre patch of tomatoes, with plants six feet apart in twelve foot rows, yet the vines overlapped in the rows and the fruit were so large that most of them packed 96 to a crate, with some too big to ship. When they matured he kept all three boats busy hauling them to market.

John finally sold the N. B. BROWARD I to the Southern States Land and Timber Co. to be used for excursion trips, but she burned in 1920, and the HERMINE he traded to Capt. Ed. Forbes for ten acres of land at Bare Beach. On one of his island farms, John built a two story store building on the canal, which he ran himself. When the lake came up in 1924 it covered his floor, so John laid planks on boxes in the aisle, but the lake kept on coming

John Aunapu's Store on Burd Island during high water.

up so he put more boxes on top of them, which caused the customers to walk slightly doubled up, but he at last traded the store to Lodi Greer for some choice lots in the newly platted townsite of Belle Glade.

In the huricane of 1928 in which lake water reached a height of 11.8 feet over the island, of the 23 people who took refuge in his packing house only 13 survived. John and his family had climbed onto his dredge when it had got loose and smashed into their house, and they were unhurt, but only a few months later, John, while tending his drainage pump one night, got tangled in the belts and was crushed to death, and that was a sad end for a mighty fine man. Ross Winne, the hardboiled deputy sheriff, when he found him, blubbered like a baby and the rest of us felt like crying too.

But I was going to tell you how John Aunapu got his farming done. He was going to defy tradition and import negroes to the lake, but folks all said it wouldn't work. Negroes had a mortal terror of the lake, for they had heard that the catfishermen would kill any who showed their faces there. Several had gone up to the lake and never returned and that enough for them. A tale had gone around that Big Foot Bill had hired a negro deckhand once, and that when the negro dropped the anchor overboard without any rope attached, Bill had tossed him over after it. Now, that was just a legend but it got around. But Wright Shackleford,who made trips around the lake to pick up his empty gasoline drums from all those fish camps, had once lost his negro deckhand from the barge during a storm, and also, right in Ft. Lauderdale, Ziegler's deckhand had fallen into the river and was pulled under by the paddlewheel, and so they would have none of the lake.

But John needed labor and he didn't despair. He knew right well that no crew of negroes would remain after the first payday unless they had their three principal requisites of life, namely and to wit: women, whiskey and gambling. To be sure, liquor would be no problem at all for those woods abounded in moonshine stills. To handle the gambling he engaged the services of one Snake Eyes, a suave ebony operator said to be the most accomplished gambler in Lauderdale. With Snake Eyes' help he then made arrangements with Seldom Seen, a young, buxom and popular wench, and a couple of her brunette friends, Jookin Kate and Big Laig Liz, to come along and add some zip to the expedition. With these attractions for bait, John eventually got a crew of 150 men. The shiners furnished liquor, Snake Eyes kept them broke, the girls kept them from getting lonesome, John got his land cleared and planted, and if everybody wasn't happy, I'll be durned if I know why not.

CHAPTER FOURTEEN

Freighters on the Lake

During those years when Aunapu and Ziegler and Big
Foot Bill were freighting down to Lauderdale, a shorter
route to civilization was provided when the unfinished
Palm Beach Canal was opened in 1917. This cut the
distance by one third, and this canal was deeper,too,
but when you reached the coast you still hadn't got nowhere. Boats docked down near the railroad bridge, midway between Lake Worth and West Palm Beach, then
everything had to be trucked to the depot in town, four
miles way. Later on West Palm Beach got smart and
dug a narrow stub canal to a turning basin at Okeechobee Road and Lake Avenue, to which the railroad
built a spur. The basin is there yet, a pretty lake in the
city park, but then it was a cussed mile or more from
the nearest store or even from a telephone. In Ft. Lauderdale, on the other hand, boats tied up at the railroad
dock beside the depot, and I'm not lying to you, you
wouldn't have to walk more than two blocks to reach
any store in town. So that was the reason that freight
boats ran to Lauderdale just as long as they could possibly make that trip.

As settlers on the lake increased, so did freight boats
too, till they were thicker than chizzywinks around a
lantern, but yet it seemed there never were enough if

you had a batch of tomatoes about to rot there on your dock.

One of the first freighters to use the Palm Beach canal and about the last to quit this run was Capt. John Grey's BERNICE. She had been built by Bill Eastman, a fisherman from Sarasota, who had run her and his PILOT'S BRIDE to Lauderdale until the war, when Grey bought her for the Palm Beach run. BERNICE was 64 feet 11 inches long, butt headed (square bowed to you), and had a four cylinder 25 horse engine, and she could carry a powerful heavy load. Usually Capt. Grey ran the boat himself but at times her skipper might be Pat Carrol, Bill Byd or John Fultz. Fultz once attached the boat for back wages and tried operating her himself, but I guess he didn't make an out of it, for creditors tied her up at Canal Point with a sheriff's attachment. There she stayed, with Pat Carrol for caretaker, until the storm in 1928 wrecked her on the beach.

Let me tell you about the old RED ROVER, Captain Thompson's schooner, which he brought to Pelican Lake

Captain John Grey's BERNICE loading at Canal Point.

about in 1902 and which ran fish to Ft. Myers in the early days. J. P. Heimer bought her from Homer Hand who had remodelled her for carrying freight. Heimer already owned the MINNESOTA, which was run by Leo Maxwell and Carl Cone until she burned at the mouth of Big Mound canal. The boys then transferred to the RED ROVER and ran her till she was sold to a fish company on the Gulf. But it wasn't the RED ROVER'S fault that she was banished from the lake. It was on account of a mess of English peas. A broker at Canal Point had bought 1300 hampers of peas from the Florida Sugar and Food Products Co., for which he paid $5000 in cash. This figured out at $3.80 a hamper, a right good price, but the broker knew what he was doing, for peas in New York were worth $7.00 then. That night Maxwell and Cone cranked up the old RED ROVER and started for Moore Haven in the teeth of a stiff north-wester, towing those high priced peas in a covered barge. They

QUEEN OF THE LAKE in Clewiston's Industrial Canal. First Owned by I. H. Stone of Bare Beach, who Sold Her to Clewiston Development Company.

had put a negro in the barge to keep her pumped out, but of course, negro like, he feel asleep. Before they had reached Observation Island, Cone looked back and to his horror saw the barge awash, with hampers of peas strowed out a mile astern. The negro was still on the barge hollering like mad. Of course, in those days, nobody carried insurance, so Heimer had to pay for the peas, which together with losing the MINNESOTA a couple of years before, sort of put him on the rocks. He sold the RED ROVER and got a job at the White Belt Dairy in Hialeah, and I reckon the only ones who profited were some fishermen who picked up and sold the drowned peas.

The RED ROVER was old, but so was the CORONA. This hoary headed wet-tail steamboat had been built by Capt. Ben. F. Hall who had sold her to the Menges, who sold her to Tom Bass, and then she was bought by Carl Cone's grandfather, Capt. Peter Cone. Like Capt. Norman Fitzhugh, he was an old steamboat hand from the St. Johns. For eight years he had carried mail from Jacksonville up to Sanford and for sixteen years to Palatka, and had found time besides to be sheriff of Volusia County. During these years he had operated the big steamers FEARLESS and ALLIGATOR as well as the gasoline powered LUCILLE.

In 1917 Peter Cone made a few trips in the CORONA from Lauderdale to the lake, then took her to Cocoa for overhaul, where he replanked the hull, flared her bows and installed Cone's safety boiler, patented by his son Percy, and then put her on the Indian River run. But a bridge was built at Eau Gallie and trucks now could haul the oranges from the beach, so Cone brought the old CORONA back to Okeechobee to haul supplies and vegetables till, like the BERNICE, she was wrecked at Canal Point in 1928.

More than likely you'll remember seeing, across the street from Pahokee's bank, a strange, two story, eight

sided house with a lookout tower on top. Well, it was
brought there from Cocoa by Peter Cone. The story goes
that this structure had been built by some rogue of a
smuggler whose conscience bothered him no doubt, for
he didn't want any corners that an enemy could hide
behind. The main reason being, so 'tis said, that he en-
joyed having several wives at once and all of them might
not be his own. And so I say, gosh, what a man!

N o w, Peter Cone, while still in the Indian River
orange trade had built himself the 80 foot, gasoline powered INDIAN RIVER, a twin screw boat, although her
wide, overhanging guards or gunnels gave her the appearance of a river steamer. On this boat, as on the
CORONA, the crew more than likely consisted of three
generations of Cones. Old Peter, of course was captain.
His son Percy, later engineer on the big dredge R. P.
CLARK, was engineer, while grandson Carl was firemen
or roustabout.

Cone finally traded the INDIAN RIVER to Pahokee's promoter B. A. Howard for ten acres near the
present negro school. Howard then sold her to Ray
Shackford, who owned the launch ELLA MAY and a

CORONA as she looked when owned by Menge Brothers.

couple of barges. Shackford then installed a single 24x
24 inch propeller and a 125 horse Standard engine and
changed her name to MAUDE. But Shackford blame
near lost his boat when he tangled with a waterspout.
Coming from Moore Haven one dark night with 125
drums of gasoline, off Observation Island this huge
waterspout seized his boat and spun her like a top. The
deadwood under her stern was wrenched until water
poured in the garboard seam to the thickness of a man's
hand. With the hand bilge pump and a three inch pump
run by the engine, they kept afloat till they beached her
at Canal Point. She was repaired and hauled gasoline
again, till like so many other boats, she was finished
by the hurricane in 1928.

Another gasoline hauling boat was the MAY E. of
the Moore Haven Zimmermans, who ran a fleet of boats
under the name of Lake Shore Transportation Co. Their
ELMO carried general freight between lake points, and
so did their BAY ISLE. Now this was a huzzy of a boat.
Once she had been a sloop, but now, with a pilot house
forward and a two cylinder Murray & Tregurtha engine
whose flywheel, of all places, was behind the engine,
she was run sometimes by Zimmerman's sons, sometimes
by John Fultz or else by Dick LeFils. Her last route was
carrying mail from Clewiston to Canal Point by way of
Kreamer Island. By this time she was so old and leaky
that at the end of each day's run, the boys had to beach
her on a flat and run her propeller in reverse to fan mud
into her seams, so they'd find her afloat next morning.
But Zimmerman did have one fine boat, the SEMINOLE
QUEEN, with cabins above and below, which was a favorite for land company's excursions.

There was another gasoline-hauling boat which had
started life like a lady but ended like a tramp. This was
the ELECTRA. Once she had been a beautiful sailing
yacht carrying gay summer cruising parties on Long
Island's Great South Bay. Built in 1900 by the famous

yacht designer and builder, N. G. Herreshoff, for Horace
O. Havermeyer, she had been the pride of her builder
and the joy of her owner. She had an overall length of
56 feet and a waterline of 31, a beam of 14 foot ten
inches and three foot draft with her centerboard up. She
had a single towering mast and an awninged "summer
cabin" to shelter the ladies or for refuge from a shower.
Somehow ELECTRA had wandered to Miami, where the
Torry fisherman, Emmet McLaughlin discovered her dor-
mant and forlorn, and bought her pretty cheap. I reckon
he got her cheap. After he'd sold her spars and the lead
from her keel she had repaid him for his investment!
Emmet cut her length to 45 feet, put in a 12 horse Grey
engine, built a horrible cabin on deck and put her on the
Lauderdale to lake freight run. Then she was bought
by Ray Shackford who put her to hauling drums of
gasoline and oil from Okeechobee to Moore Haven. Her
Captain Davis must have been a Scotchman, for he
thriftily drained enough gas from supposedly empty drums
to keep his own engine going.

Zimmerman's SEMINOLE QUEEN at Moore Haven.

L. Francis Herreshoff, her builder's son, had said of
the ELECTRA, "She was a beautiful yacht and it is a
shame that she was ever changed into a freight boat".
But that's life I guess, so have your fun when you are
young, for some day you may have to go to work.

One of the big freight boats was RITTA I., and she
looked a heap bigger even than she was. Her tall, housed-
in cargo space rose above a high sided hull, and was
topped off by cabins behind a lofty pilot house. With
her shallow draft she must have been a dilly to handle
in a beam wind. She was a sternwheeler, but not a steamboat, for her engine was a 15 horse stationary Fairbanks-
Morse. I reckon that she was intended to be called the
RITTA ISLAND, but everybody, not even excusing her
own crew, always called her RITTA EYE. She had been
built in 1918 by the Bare Beach men, O. M. Revels, who
owned a general store, and Hector Harris, who ran her,
and was county commissioner as well.

During the season of 1921 while Joe Johnson was her
skipper and Bill Hunt her engineer, Bare Beach had such
a bumper crop of Irish potatoes that the boat hauled
them to West Palm Beach for six solid weeks without a
stop for breath, and the crew never got to sleep in bed.
But that was freighting, brother!

Once while anchored off Bare Beach a storm came
up. The RITTA I. dragged her anchor and fetched up
in a hog pen ashore. After the wind tide went down you
could have walked around her dry footed, and most
folks thought she'd be a landmark there, but Gus Mc-
Gehee, a Ritta Island homesteader and boatman, allowed
as how he'd get her afloat again. He waited a few weeks
for another good north-wester, set out a couple of anchors in tandem, and with a rope to that stationary
engine's nigger head he got her into the lake again, and
for that he got her skipper's job. Up till 1923 she made
weekly trips to West Palm Beach until she was sold for
hauling oranges at Bonita Springs, and there, not a

month later, she caught fire from an upset lantern and burned to the water's edge.

The building of Conners Highway gave work to lots of boats. One was the tug ANDRAE, first brought to the lake by Southern Fisheries. On the highway job she was run by Buck Tillman. After that was finished Frank O'Connell and Leo Maxwell hauled pilings and lumber with her for building the Highway 70 bridge across Kissimmee River.

There was another tug, a sternwheeler, which sunk in the lake, and if she's ever been found, I've never heard of it, though I've asked of many a person. This was the SKIMMER, built in 1910 in Galveston for the Furst-Clark Construction Company. Steel Hulled, she was, 61.4x18.2 in size and she drew only two foot seven. Her big paddle wheel was turned by a single cylinder Fairbanks Morse, and she had so little freeboard that when she was under way, you'd swear her hull was under water. On her last trip, in the summer of 1917, she was coming from Ft. Lauderdale to the St. Lucie Canal to tend the dredge R.P.

RITTA I. at a Little Bare Beach Picnic.

CLARK. Arthur Davis was her captain, while his brother Fred was engineer. About three miles offshore from Port Mayaca she ran into a most bodacious squall and foundered out of sight. Both men got ashore, but she'd gone down in the deepest part of the lake, maybe in one of those pot holes the seiners used to tell about, and so far as I can learn, she was never seen again.

Oh, there were a slush of other freighters too, Capt. Bass' LE HAVEN, Lockmiller's SOUTH BAY, Harmon Raulerson's steamer SUCCESS built for Tom Bass in 1906, which hauled tomatoes here in 1924, and—oh yes, I like to have forgot the launch BORNETTA with her covered barge. Her crew was something different for the lake. David Hilderman and his wife owned and ran the rig. They had come from a German speaking part of Russia to Saskatchewan in Canada, and then by way of Micco Landing on the Kissimmee, down here to Little Bare Beach, where they had tried to farm a while. From 1917 to 1920 they hauled vegetables to West Palm Beach, and brother, to see that good lady, head and ears tied down with a red bandanna and her wide skirts a-flying in the breeze as she pumped out her barge way out there in the lake, might give you quite a shock at first, and she didn't mind handling those crates and hampers either.

And there were store boats too, in the early days of settlers on the lake. The first one was the powered sloop of J. M. Baker, pioneer storekeeper at Okeelanta, which delivered groceries to Glade Crest down the Hillsboro canal, and then to Ritta, where he supplied Maud Wingfield till she got big enough to buy direct. But the main store boat was J. R. Poland's BISCAYNE which voyaged around the lake as early as 1915 and 1916 to all the fish camps and settlers too. She was a regular floating store. You could tell her by that A tent on top which covered her packaged merchandise. Grover Kelly or Red McLendon ran the boat but Poland did the selling till he retired to farm on East Beach.

There even was a church boat on the lake, the 32 foot EVANGEL I, of the Congregational Board of Home Missions, captained by the Rev. Charles E. Enlow. He called his boat the Gospel Navy. She tied up at my Okeelanta dock a couple of times before the war, with her little organ, and flying a white pennant with a red cross. But she didn't seem to spend too much time around the lake. When it came to saving souls I reckon those catfishers and freight boat men weren't scarcely worth the effort.

But of all the boats which cruised the lake and travelled the Everglades canals, there was none so well known as the State's boat TRANSIT, for she went everywhere, and did they keep her looking like a yacht! Built in 1914 in Jacksonville, her cypress hull was 40 feet long with 10 foot beam and had berths for ten men. She drew 26 inches of water and could make ten knots if they could find water deep enough, which seldom happened. She might be carrying a survey party or a construction crew, but just as likely she might have the state's chief engineer, its treasurer, attorney general, or maybe the governor himself. After a couple of decades of this she was sold to become a tugboat. Like the ELEC-TRA, she had to go to work.

Now that I've told you of all the boats that sailed this lake, you'll naturally ask, how did we find our way about. What did we have for buoys and beacons and lights?

Since the days of Capt. Ben F. Hall and J. Fred Menge, boats by the hundreds had sailed the lake, steamboats, runboats, passenger and freight boats with now and again a big floating dredge, yet the only aids to navigation were the occasional cypress trees which towered above the shoreline swamp. To be sure, the Flat Top Cypress had once had a flag, and later on a barrel in its branches to mark Three Mile Canal, and the Okeelanta settlers, getting tired of being lost in the lake at night, prevailed on a squatter on the shore to hoist a lantern every night to show the entrance to the canal to Lauderdale. But it was not till the winter of 1915-16 that the U. S. Lighthouse Service discovered Lake Okeechobee, when they installed fifteen beacons, some of them with lights, at the entrance to canals and on some reefs. By 1927, counting those in Lake Hicpochee, the number had increased to 22, and that was mighty fine. The only objection was, by that time there were no boats.

But I was about to forget the last freight boat line of all. It, like the first passenger line to cross the state, was operated by a Forbes, Edwin E., the brother of Felix. He had organized a family concern, the South Shore Transportation Company, consisting of himself, his brother-in-law H. C. Willits the financier, Ed's boys Charlie and Jack, and Ed's son-in-law, William Rawls. They all lived in South Bay. Starting in 1924, their cabin boats FOX and ARLINE G. carried mail and passengers from Clewiston to Belle Glade and down the canal to the Brown Farm at Shawano. Their 75 foot ESTERO, bought from Korashian Unity Assn., hauled Texaco products and general freight from Clewiston to Okeechobee. They had lost no boats in the hurricane of '28, but completion of the highway from South Bay to Clewiston made the last link in roads around the lake, and that, my friend, spelled the end of commercial boating on this lake.

And now, although it has nothing to do with boats, let's take a look at Capt. Ed Forbes' farming experience, not that it was unusual. No! It was just an example of what those early farmers were up against, more especially if they tried to farm the islands. It will show you that there was not much pie in the pioneering, and that's a stomped down fact.

Frosts and freezes, and rabbits too, could do a heap of damage, but that no one could prevent. It was the water situation that hurt the worst, and for that the Internal Improvement Board and state engineers got most of the blame. But we should give the devil and the engineers their due. They couldn't help long periods of drouth nor months when the rains forgot to stop. The original plan to drain the Everglades at one fell swoop was no good from the start. The "war on the Everglades" had stopped the sale of lands and meant no funds for work. To be sure, during the wet '20's the state had built a levee to protect the south shore's farms, but that meant that the islanders, who had the finest land of all, were about to grow web feet. The fishermen and boatmen wanted the lake kept high. So did those who wanted water for irrigation and to flood the sawgrass lands so they wouldn't catch fire and burn. Lakeshore farmers craved to have it low to prevent flooding of their crops. Farmers down the Caloosahatchee and on the East Coast too, raised heck when lake water drowned their crops and groves. It was sure a fouled up situation.

But Ed Forbes says, and I think he's right, that always the state seemed to do its job just backwards. In a dry season the engineers would lower the lake, and when it rained they raised it.

Now, Ed had been farming his homestead on Ritta Island and did right well until that levee was built. For three years then it was too wet, so he rented some land at Bare Beach from the sugar company for 1/7 of the yield. He had his choice of land in the sub-drainage district, which was low, or of high land outside of it. This happened to be in a dry period when high land was dried out, full of cracks and hard as coal, so naturally he chose low ground, and that's where he made a humbug. It started to rain and rain and rain and the district couldn't pump off all the water. His tractor stayed bogged down in the field and he raised nothing all that winter. So he hired a dredge and diked his island land but storms melted the dike like sugar. Floods and frosts had kept his freight boat customers from paying him their bills so he owed a heap of bills himself. So that's how come he sold his island land to R. Y. Creech right cheap, before the fertilizer company could foreclose its mortgage, and he left the Glades to live in town.

Ed recently told me that he had pioneered already in two Western states and thought it pretty tough, but the hardships and discouragements out west had been nothing to what people here had endured in these Everglades of Florida. "I wouldn't go through it again for a milion dollars cash!" and to that, I'll bet, many another old settler would shout "Amen brother!"

CHAPTER FIFTEEN

The Real McCoy

By this time you're beginning to suspect that we had some right interesting characters running boats on this old lake, but I haven't told you of Bill McCoy. He like to have topped them all. He got world famous at any rate.

During those days when traffic was getting heavy on the Ft. Lauderdale canal, a shorter route to civilization was opened when boats could run to West Palm Beach through the unfinished Palm Beach canal in 1917. The first passenger boat to use this route was Capt. Bass' OBSERVATION, a 45 foot cabin and canopy boat run by Harry Loy. She carried passengers from the coast to Canal Point and across to Moore Haven, and she had the mail route too, until Fitzhugh got that contract. Then, after Conners Highway was finished, she carried mail under sub-contract from Canal Point to Pahokee, Bacom Point and Kreamer Island until she was sold to Clewiston's promoters.

But the OBSERVATION hadn't been long on the Palm Beach canal till she had stiff competition from the McCoy brothers, William P. and Benjamin F., who had been building boats at Holly Hill, up Daytona way. The McCoys brought their glass cabin EAGLE and EIGHT BELLS with fancy striped awnings, and allowed

143

as how they would take care of the tourist business, they wouldn't fool with freight. Each day one boat left from Bunker's Landing on the canal near West Palm Beach, and the other from Moore Haven, passing each other at Canal Point. The fare was only two dollars, and business got so good that they added the new and faster CROCODILE which could make ten miles an hour in the lake. After Conners Highway was opened they ran their own bus from West Palm Beach to Canal Point, while at Moore Haven they connected with the Clark Line bus to the west coast, so now, with the Florida Transportation Company's six bus a day schedules between Miami and West Palm Beach, they could advertise "Breakfast in Miami, Dinner on Lake Okeechobee and Supper in Ft. Myers". Cross state travel sure was picking up. For special charters they used the big CONSTITUTION which they had built in Holly Hill in 1909. She surely was an impressive craft, 75 feet by 18, with double decks and sleeping accommodations f o r sixty

OBSERVATION unloading at Canal Point.

passengers. She was finally sold to Clewiston's Issaac
T. Cook, who changed her name to POLLY ANNA III.
What's left of her can still be seen there in the Industrial
Canal. Ben was manager of the McCoy line and he got
the business, too, leastwise until highways and railroads
got too numerous, when he closed out in May 1925.

But I started out to tell you about Ben's brother,
Bill McCoy. Now there was much of a man, standing
six feet two, with shoulders like a cargo hatch, a punch
like a sledge hammer and a most engaging smile. Bill
craved excitement and this humdrum canal navigation
was about to get him down, so when he was near about
forty years old he decided to win some fame and for-
tune by running booze from the Bahamas, and succeeded beyond his fondest expectations. Rum running was
something new to Bill but the sea was not, for he had
served in yachts and merchant ships and had been mate
in the Key West to Havana steamer OLIVET.

Bill started out by buying the Gloucester schooner
HENRY L. MARSHALL in which he sailed from Nassau
with 1500 cases of rye, which he put ashore near Savannah without being caught, the first and only time he
unloaded in the U. S. waters. For this load he received
$15,000, which blame near paid for his ship on her
first trip. His next venture was to carry 1500 cases of
rye and Scotch from Nassau to New York for a gang
just getting started. After anchoring off Far Rocka-
way he slipped ashore and was plumb disgusted to find
out that the buyers had never given a thought as to
how they'd get the liquor ashore. "Do I have to show
you guys how to do everything?" he demanded, as he
stomped out to find the owners of some small boats
who'd like to earn a few quick bucks. So this made Bill
and his MARSHALL the ones to found Rum Row, that
anchored fleet of schooners, yachts, square riggers, rus-
ty tramps and old sub chasers which eventually stretch-

ed from Montauk Point to Cape May in New Jersey.
Every night, unless it blew a hurricane, seaskiffs by
the scores streaked out to load and smuggle in the high
priced merchandise.

McCoy's swift schooners with liquor legally bought
in Nassau, Bermuda, Halifax or St. Pierre would anchor
well offshore in international waters and sell their stock
quite legally on the high seas for cash. Bill's ships, un-
like a small minority of others, never varied their
method by smuggling dope or Chinamen. By the summer
of 1923 Bill's reputation for square dealing and for handling nothing but best quality and unadulterated liquor was
so well established that New York buyers scrambled to
unload his boats. In his fast Gloucester schooner ARE-
THUSA, renamed TOMOKA, he was making regular
trips from Nassau to Rum Row, three weeks for the
round trip, almost to the day. Bill was making money,
but to him it was a game, himself against an unpopular
law, but he tried to play it square. Bribery, hi-jacking
and double crossing were not for him. He said afterward "I never gave nor took a dirty dollar!" and since
the liquor which he sold was nothing but first quality
and uncut, it earned the nickname of "The Real Mc-
Coy".

Bill's reputation for strict honesty served him mighty
well and was reciprocated by his customers. On Rum
Row the seaskiff men would hand him rolls of thousand
dollar bills which he never counted till afterward, then
load their boats from his hold themselves, yet he was
never shorted a case of liquor nor a dollar. After he
had once rescued a crew of hi-jackers from drowning
and entertained them for the night, even that unprinci-
pled class of gentry left his boats strictly alone. One
mob had even boarded one of his schooners and held
up the crew, but when they learned the ship was Bill
McCoy's they apologized and shoved off. Another time
a crew of pirates even took the trouble to ask him if he

had really sold a certain ship before they dashed away to hi-jack her. The captains and crews of the Revenue cutters and the Treasury agents who pursued him, although he loved to embarrass them, gave him a grudging respect.

Bill McCoy was making money and he was having fun. Sailing his ARETHUSA was his greatest pleasure, but Bill was having his troubles, too. His skipper and trusted friend, Albert Gott, died of a heart attack. Another true friend, Captain J. Crosby was killed in a storm by a falling tackle block. His J. B. YOUNG was run down and badly damaged by a steamer, the MARSHALL and the M. M. GARDNER had strayed into U. S. waters and were captured. He was kept busy bailing out his captured boats and seamen, and before he quit, his lawyers had nicked him for quarter of a million.

As time went on the government kept getting tougher, organized mobs using graft and bribes to gain political power were taking over. It was becoming a dirty, crooked business and Bill was beginning to wish he was out of it. He soon got his wish, for he now was the number one most wanted man of the U. S. government.
Although McCoy had been one of the biggest contributors to the booming prosperity of Nassau and Halifax and had made the sleepy fishing village of St. Pierre a busy port, yet the British government, chief benefactor of the liquor trade, had secretly agreed that it would make no objection if Bill McCoy, in his British ship, should be taken into custody on the high seas, British flag or no. So it came to pass that the cutter SENECA, after an exciting chase, while lobbing shells which kept hitting closer, overhauled and captured McCoy in his ARETHUSA on November 20, 1923. It was all highly illegal but it worked. Bill was arrested and put under $15,000 bond. He was accused of all kinds of assorted

skullduggery, including bribing treasury agents, which
he denied, and firing on the United States flag, which
in one manner of speaking might have been true. Once
some Coast Guard men in an unlighted boat had sneaked
alongside one night, so Bill's crew fired a volley over
their heads thinking they were a gang of hi-jackers.
He appeared before innumerable hearings, listening to
indictments not strong enough to take to court, and yet,
for sixteen months they wouldn't turn him loose, while
lawyers meanwhile bled him white. At last he pleaded
guilty to a charge, expecting to get off with a fine, but
the government was determined to put him behind the
bars. Before the judge sentenced him, a treasury agent,
Pete Sullivan, asked the court's permission to speak a
word. In his Irish brogue he related how, while on a
trip to Nassau for the purpose of nabbing Bill, he had
been recognized by some rum runners who prepared
to rub him out. Just then McCoy had appeared, claimed Sullivan as an old friend and customer, and shipped
him safely back to the states, which undoubtedly saved
his life.

Instead of being sentenced to the pen for the rest
of his natural life, Bill got nine months in the local jail,
but since the warden's name was McGuinness, the chief
keeper's name was Reilly, the doctor was a Murphy
and the sheriff was McConnell, I reckon that a McCoy
there didn't fare too bad.

CHAPTER SIXTEEN

Ed Kettner and His Camels

"I'd walk a mile for a Camel!" Did you ever wonder who first said that? Well, I knew the man and so did you, if you've been around these Everglades very long. He was one of the first men to drive a bus from coast to coast, and much of a man he was, for sure. Ed Kettner was his name. But first, just let me give you some idea of what bus travel here was like in Ed Kettner's day.

Before Conners Highway, from the East Coast to Lake Okeechobee, had been finished in 1924, cross state travel had mostly been by boat. Fitzhugh's mail and passenger boat PALM and the boats of the McCoy brothers too, had run from West Palm Beach up the canal to Canal Point, then thirty miles across the lake to Moore Haven. Here Fitzhugh's passengers transferred to the Hand Brothers Boat and Bus Company's boats and at LaBelle to their busses to Ft. Myers. Of course, after the opening of Conners Highway, both Fitzhugh and the McCoys used busses on that part of their runs too.

Belle Glade also, at the same time, began to get some bus service to West Palm Beach, since the branch road from there to Twenty Mile Bend had just been finished also. This bus was nothing but a passenger car and it was run by H. M. Walters, nephew of Tom Walters, one of Belle Glade's first settlers. It was not till 1926 that this Belle Glade road was extended to Pahokee and Canal Point in one direction, and to South Bay in the other, and it was three more crying years before it ever reached to Clewiston. During that time the only road along the lake's south shore had been a mucky trail winding between custard apple trees, head high elders, and in summer, pigweeds twenty feet in height. In dry weather clouds of itchy muck dust could coat you blacker than a Nassau negro. After rains you'd surely get bogged down. Canals could be crossed on little pontoon floats attached by chains to each bank. Naturally, the float was probably tied fast to the opposite bank, but after stripping off, swimming across and pumping the blamed thing out, the crossing was no trouble. No trouble at all, that is, unless some low rogue had borrowed the float to move a tractor and had left it five miles down the canal.

The state finally got the Huffman Construction Company to build a highway on this South Bay-to-Clewiston stretch. The grade (all muck, of course) was partly

Ferry Barge, Used before Bridges Were Built. Okeelanta 1920.

finished in the spring of 1929 when I took a notion to journey over to Clewiston. The car was an open Dodge sedan, one of the first to use low pressure tires. Sometimes we'd drive on top of the unleveled grade, sometimes alongside in the boggy road. We'd bounce and jolt and skid. Only by holding a death grip on the top bow overhead could I stay in that blasted car at all. Every time the wheels would spin and threaten to bog down, the driver would heave a mighty sigh and exclaim, "Gosh, if we didn't have baloon tires we never could have pulled out that time!" That same year the hurricane washed a goodly potion of that grade away, so for the next few months travel was a right smart worse I reckon, if such were possible.

Then too, the road from Clewiston to Moore Haven and on to Ft. Myers was nothing much to brag of either, partly muck, partly sand, some parts graded but a right smart not. The Hand brothers, Homer and Oscar, drove a couple of busses with home made bodies, an Overland and a Reo Speed Wagon. Their Sundays were mostly spent in patrolling this sandy trail, spreading palmetto fans in the rutted spots and tossing more saplings and sawmill slabs into the worst bogs and sloughs. In this way they hoped to keep on running near about on schedule for another week.

Meanwhile, over on the Gulf Coast, Barron G. Collier, owner of most of Collier County, in order to promote his property, had been running a fleet of five boats between Tampa, Ft. Myers and his little town of Everglade. When a new highway, the Tamiami Trail, connected these towns, he began to operate busses and freight trucks instead, and that was the beginning of the Tamiami Trail Tours, Inc. Also, he decided to try extending his activities eastward, so the T.T.T. bought out Fitzhugh's boat and bus. The old PALM continued to run across the lake for a spell, but the water got too shoal for her to put into Clewiston. To remedy this situation and to give service to other south shore towns and settlements, the T.T.T. started a bus run all the way from Ft. Myers to West Palm Beach. This bus, we'd just as well admit it now, was nothing but a Willys Knight sedan. Her driver was Wayne M. Cox, and he's superintendent of transportation for the same T.T.T. right now. Cox used to run his bus from Ft. Myers, crossing the Caloosahatchee at LaBelle, then stopping at Ortona (which is principally a cemetery now), Citrus Center (there's not a vestige of that town today), Moore Haven and Clewiston. From there he could travel the newly finished road to South Bay, then to Belle Glade, Pahokee, Canal Point and to West Palm Beach.

Howsomeever, this new run must not have appeared to them as a smart idea, for the company turned it over to Ed and Mary Kettner, charging them only $1 a year for the privilege. Ed Kettner had been crippled when his plane crash landed in San Francisco, so with an honorable discharge from the Navy, he got himself married and migated to Florida. The Kettners made their start here by delivering newspapers and package express from West Palm Beach to Clewiston, driving that mucky, boggy south shore trail in a ¾ ton White truck, and shopping in town for their Gladeside customers, just as the freight boat men before them had been doing. Before the first year was over they were running three trucks and hauling freight as well. Yes, freight and passengers too, if they could put up with the accommodations, but then, folks couldn't be too choosy in those days.

In 1930 the Kettners quit hauling freight and went to carrying passengers only. Their bus was a station wagon with 310,000 miles and $700 mortgage, yet by October of that year their Glades K (for Kettner) Motor Line was running three station wagons, and making three round trips to Clewiston and one to Ft. Myers every day.

Now, Ed's wife Mary was a person well worth knowing too. Auburn haired, big boned like a lady wrestler, and walking with a decided limp, she was Ed's partner in the transportation business. Those first three trucks were run by Ed and Mary and by a negro named Jaybo, whom Ed would regularly pay off and fire, well knowing that Mary, just as regularly, would hire him right back again. Mary was business manager as well as bus driver too. She tried to keep her busses running somewhere near on schedule, and keep the bills paid up, not always so blooming easy in those depression years. Her special job was to get hold of the cash receipts before Ed had a chance to blow them in. Ed loved to stop his drivers on the road, get their cash fares and COD collections, and feed them into slot machines along his route. And mister, there were a heap of those slot machines.

It was while driving an empty station wagon in the edge of that famous Labor Day Hurricane of September 2, 1935 that Ed got killed. This car had a tricky steering gear. Mary wouldn't drive it herself at all. In this storm, where the road suddenly narrowed nine miles west of LaBelle, his car left the road and turned over in the ditch. A loose electric motor inside struck Ed on the head and killed him, and it was hours later before he was discovered.

But Mary wouldn't quit. She kept adding new schedules and new busses until she built up quite a fleet. Three Ford sedans were cut in two amidship and lengthened to 210 inch wheelbase, so naturally they were known as "stretch-outs". Then she got a $15,000 Flexible coach, factory built, with engine in the rear, luggage rack on top, seats for twenty-five passengers, and believe it or not—with air conditioning, well, at least sometimes. And besides, she had a couple of passenger cars for special trips or for "doubling" on regular runs.

In 1941, with the opening of the new highway from South Bay to Ft. Lauderdale, then known as State Road 25 and otherwise as Thomas E. Will Memorial Highway, Mary succeeded in getting the coveted exclusive franchise to run that route. But by this time Mary had driven her own busses herself one million miles and she decided to retire. She leased, then later sold, her franchises and rolling stock to another husband-and-wife team, Carl and Verda Weaver from Lakeland, who took the name of Glades Motor Lines. During the war years the Weavers ran five round trips a day from West Palm Beach to Belle Glade, four to Ft. Myers, two to Lakeland and four from Belle Glade to Miami. On November 1, 1948 the Weavers sold their company to the same outfit which had started this cross state run, Tamiami Trail Tours, which is still running these same routes, and more too, to this day.

But I was fixing for to tell you about Ed Kettner and his camels. Now, Ed could tell some of the most bodacious stories about his past adventures, though to be sure, sometimes fact and fancy seemed to get a bit confused. I'll just pass along the information as I've heard Ed tell it.

Ed claimed that he'd been in the Spanish American war and had been eleven years in the U. S. Navy and travelled three times around the world. And he was a flyer too. After Charles A. Lindbergh had made the first solo flight across the Atlantic, it was Ed's boast that he was the man who had taught Lindbergh how to fly. Ed also loved to brag that when the famous NC4 under Commander Read, had made the first airplane crossing of the Atlantic in 1919, he had been a member of the crew. That was a good story too, but somehow the Navy's official roster, which I've just checked, some-how seems to leave him out.

But now let's get back to the Camel slogan. At this late date even the tobacco company can't tell how it got started, but Ed's brother, and Mary too, claim this one tale is true. This happened back during World War I when Ed had just returned to his base from a combat flight, with his plane right tolerably well shot up. As he climbed down from the cockpit some men approach-ed him and one of them, a civilian, remarked,

"It looks as though you've had a pretty rugged flight! How'd you like to have a smoke?"

As he noticed the American cigarettes which the man had offered, Ed's eyes lighted up with joy.

"Oh, they're Camels! That's my favorite smoke. I'd walk a mile to get a Camel!"

Now, as fate and luck would have it, the stranger was an official of the R. J. Reynolds Tobacco Co., the maker of that brand. Ed's off hand remark had hit the man just right. He used it as a slogan for the cigarette, and Ed Kettner became the richer by $500.

One Little Water Hyacinth

Did you notice the same item that I was reading the other day? Some dumb, lightning struck knocker is importing piranhas from the Amazon, and it's feared that they will get loose in the streams of Florida, and our U.S. Representative, Paul G. Rogers, bless his heart, is trying to put a stop to it.

Now, a piranha, in case you shouldn't know, is one of the most vicious, voracious and deadly of all the fish that swim. In their home stomping grounds it's sure death for an animal to venture into the water. Why, if a man just leans overboard to wash his hands, he'll likely lose some fingers. Goodness gracious and gee whiz! Imagine what might happen if a pair of those piranhas got loose here! Let me tell you what just one solitary import from that same region has already done. That's the water hyacinth.

I'll grant you that there's no more beautiful flower on land or sea than the water hyacinth. But brother, when you say that, you've said it all. Of course, cows love to eat the plant, but since it's 95% water, a cow can starve slam to death even with her belly full. If they are good for anything nobdy yet has found it out. Why, one foremost soil scientist, after ten years of experi-

George Graham, Okeelanta Settler, Walking across Bolles Canal on
Hyacinths.

Dr. William J. Buck, after a professional Call to Okeelanta Hotel,
Crossing North New River Canal on Hyacinths, 1932.

menting, declared at last. "The water hyacinth is not worth a damn for anything!"

Here's how they came to Florida. Back in 1884, so the story goes, a lady living on the St. Johns River visited the New Orleans International Cotton Exposition. There she was entranced by some gorgeous flowers which had come from Venezuela. Hoping to adorn her fish pond with its lavender blossoms, she purchased one single plant and hoped that it would grow in Florida. It did! It grew and kept on dividing and multiplying, a sort of arithmetic plant, so to speak. Some say she dumped the excess plants into the St. Johns River, some that she strewed from a steamboat for to beautify the stream. No matter. It wasn't long till steamboats could hardly navigate the St. Johns nor its tributaries because of her lovely plants.

And here's how they got to Lake Okeechobee. It must have been about in 1897 or '98 that Eli Morgan, a cattleman at Bassenger who later moved to Bluefields, decided to raise some cheap cow feed. He hired Bill Whidden, with his horse and wagon, to get some plants from the St. Johns and sow them in ponds and ditches around Bassenger. From there eventually, they got into every stream, every pond, and every canal in South Florida. And still they kept on multiplying. Scientists will tell you that a hyacinth divides itself and doubles in number in only two weeks time. In eight months one plant will produce 65,000 more, and the only natural enemies it has are freezing weather and salt water.

Soon water-flow in rivers and canals was slowed by one half. Streams and ditches were clogged completely. Their oxygen cut off, most fish except for gars and mud fish died off. Fish camps and tourist spots closed up. Transportation on many rivers and canals simply ceased. In 1949 the state Game and Fresh Water Fish Commission estimated that hyacinths had cost this state $10 million in that one year alone.

Sometimes those pesky plants would be jammed so tight that a man could walk on them. In 1921 I was operating a passenger boat from Ft. Lauderdale to the lake. At the lock gate in Chosen I had barely managed to force the boat through the hyacinth jam. A Seminole tried to follow in his dugout canoe, but the cussed plants closed in and he couldn't make it. The lock tender's sons, Hans and Fritz Stein, hopped down to help, and the three of them, standing on the hyacinths, picked up the heavy boat and shoved it along on top of the plants.

Taylor Creek, once one of the busiest streams in the state, was particularly plagued with hyacinths. During the building of Conners Highway, Buck Tillman, in the tug ANDRAE, left from Okeechobee City with two 90 foot barges loaded with bridge girders and drums of gasoline. The hyacinths collected under the barges till he could hardly reach the open lake. Even then they stayed under the barges' bottoms in spite of all he did

Taylor Creek choked with Hyacinths

to shake them loose. It took him forty-eight hours to make the twenty-five mile trip to the St. Lucie canal.

Mrs. Wes Raulerson in Okeechobee recalls how her father, with his family, once left from their home on Lake Istokpoga in his launch. For two days and nights they battled the hyacinths in the creek and in Kissimmee River. Gasoline and food both gave out and mosquitoes nearly ate them up before a steamboat came along.

At Lake Harbor once during a flood time, I saw hyacinths jammed against the spillway and locks. The current kept washing more plants under those already there and raising them until they were piled like haystacks, ten feet in the air.

And talking about jams, here's a story which was told me not long ago by Bennie A. Williams of Savannah, Georgia. I know the story's true for I was right there and saw most of it myself. Williams was working on Scott Holloway's dredge which had just finished a job at Geerworth and had moved through the Bolles Canal to Okeelanta, and was bound down the North New River Canal to Ft. Lauderdale. This was in the fall of 1924 when the Glades was experiencing one of its worst floods. The canal was full of hyacinths coming down with the swift current. At the Temporary Locks, 36 miles from Ft. Lauderdale, they had formed a jam above the spillway and locks, although the lock gates were wide open. The jam already was backed up for a good quarter of a mile and was increasing in size and density every hour.

I had arrived here in the powerful tug LEVIATHAN which had always succeeded in ramming its way up Taylor Creek, even when some other boats couldn't make it. In tow were two houseboats. In one of them was the very sick wife of one of the men from a different dredging outfit on the lake. In spite of all my bucking, twisting and maneuvering, the only direction that

I could go was sideways. I knew that if the boat was forced against the bank I could never pull away, so regretfully, I managed to back out. Then I had to take the sick woman all the way to Canal Point, where she was put into a car for West Palm Beach. But before I left that jam I had walked clear around my tug on hyacinths and never wet my feet.

While I had still been there at the locks, here came the dredge outfit of Scott Holloway, an American Steel dipper dredge towing a barge of coal, and behind that their quarter boat and a launch. I decided to wait while the dredge dug a passage through the jam. In fact, I still am waiting. That dredge's heavy dipper could dig rock, but brother it couldn't dig hyacinths. When dropped, it sunk on a yielding bed and came up empty. When it did scoop up a bucketful, which sometimes happened, more plants promptly filled the hole. Pressure of the jam forced the coal barge against the bank, so in being pulled ahead it crawled up the canal

Tug LEVIATHAN Loaded with Dredge Supplies.

bank and tipped, until coal was falling over the side boards. The launch tried to pull the houseboat loose, and both finally wound up against the bank on the far side. That was when I decided that this was no place for me.

Williams later told me that they stayed here so long that their provisions gave plumb out. A yearling heifer was discovered down the canal bank and they butchered it. Later, some Seminoles arrived and furnished them with some game. Then in a small tree, six coons were discovered, so coon meat had to do for rations until a crew of engineers arrived from Lauderdale and removed the spillway to let them escape. Meanwhile all this time the crew had been walking on hyacinths to cross the canal from the dredge to the houseboat.

Captain Earl Daniels of the Arundel Corporation told me how he broke up a similar jam. This was at the railroad bridge across the Palm Beach Canal down near Lake Worth, a place I'd been to a day or two before him to get an empty barge tied to the bank just above this bridge. Fed by the big flood, the canal flowed here like a torrent. Due to the current and the hyacinths, even the LEVIATHAN couldn't budge the barge a-loose and I had to leave her there.

Daniels, with the dredge FLORIDA, was sent to break the jam. With a hawser to a tree, the dredge drifted down to the jam, which was only a few hundred feet in extent. But the steady stream of new hyacinths carried under by the savage current, caused those plants on the surface to rise in heaps and roll over in a most appalling manner. The whole mass surged and heaved. The dredge was helpless to dig, for the bucket, when dropped, actually would bounce right back.

Daniels went to town, bought a twelve foot crosscut saw and attached a piece of pipe with a cross bar for a handle. His crew then, with life lines ashore, walked onto the jam and sawed out sections which could float

Holloway's American Steel Dredge.

between the bridge's pilings. It was risky work, but he broke the jam.

Naturally, many methods have been tried to combat the hyacinths. In the Kissimmee River and in the Ever-

Dredge FLORIDA of the Arundel Corporation.

glade canals the state used to hire Captain Clay Johnson's steamer OSCEOLA to clear the channels. By
steaming backwards up the steam the paddle wheel
could break the jams and start the plants down with
the current. In Louisiana as well as in Florida, many
ingenious machines have been tried, either to chop the
plants to bits, or else to convey them to the shore. These
worked, but they were too expensive. It's even been
proposed that some other spreading plant or vine might
be introduced to smother out the plants, but it might
turn out to be another pest itself. Some one came up
with the novel idea of importing hippopotami from
Africa to eat the plants, and now by golly, they are
actually trying manatees or sea cows to see what they can
do.

So far, the only practical solution for killing the
plants came after the invention of the chemical 2-4-D
during World War II. This was devised, but never used,
for spraying the enemy's rice fields to help starve out
the Japs. Spraying 2-4-D from air planes, boats and
land machines has finally cleared hyacinths from rivers
and canals till at last you can see the water. Three or
four weeks after being sprayed the plants will die and
form a floating mass which decomposes, and after six
or eight more weeks it sinks to the bottom. Now that
would be just fine, but sometimes even after they're dead
the cussed plants will still come back to haunt you. I'll
tell you what I mean.

During the big flood in 1953 Lake Okeechobee and
the canals were higher than the land. Canals were flowing swiftly towards the coast but still the water level
kept on rising. At a spillway in New River Canal alongside Highway 27, a great mass of these dead and rotted
hyacinths had risen to the surface and formed a jam
which blocked the water flow. Working on this great
flat, black mass was a crew of six or eight negroes.
Their boss was T. G. Mayo, now with Wedgworth Farms.

They were cutting it into sections with cross cut saws, then with poles, pushing the chunks through a gap in the spillway to float farther down stream. It looked like the way people used to cut ice in ponds up north.

In 1948, after three years of 2-4-D spraying, Lamar Johnson, Chief Engineer for the Everglades Drainage District, was able to report that now 177 miles of the state's canal system had been cleared of hyacinths. The cost was $96 per mile. Since then, Dade County alone, in its own control program during the 1950's spent $76 per mile just to keep the pests in check. Farmers and other private owners still have to keep on the fight at their own expense. Nobody seems to believe that they can ever be exterminated, and only regular patrolling everywhere keeps them from getting out of hand again.

Since you've learned what one little hyacinth plant has caused, let's not experiment with piranhas!

∼∽∼∽∼∽∼∽∼∽

So now, folks, I reckon you've had a right good buzzard's eye view of transportation here when these rivers and Okeechobee Lake were new. You've learned of the smoke boats which used to fetch the oranges and gator hides to town. You've got acquainted with the power boats which brought the land buyers and first settlers to the Glades, and the freighters that carried their beans and peppers and tomatoes to the railroad docks.

Now, as you speed along the smooth highways which border the canals and rivers here, just remember the six mile an hour boats in which we used to travel, when it was a good three days round trip from this big lake to the court house in West Palm Beach. And don't forget the boatmen, too, who somehow made their trips in spite of shoals and bars and sudden squalls, in spite of hyacinths and whirlpools too. Those days we won't ever see again, but yet I'm glad I knew them too.

Sources

STEAMBOATS: Harmon Raulerson, Ray Roebuck, Grover Chandler, Lonnie Howard, *From the Gulf to the Atlantic*, Prospectus of Menge Bros. Steamboat Line, Undated; Alma Hetherington, *Those Steamboat Days*, Kissimmee Boat-A-Cade Program, 1960; J. E. Dovell, *The Development of Commercial Transportation in Florida*, Economic Leaflets, Gainesville, 1951; Kelsey Blanton, Articles on *Kissimmee River Boats*, Tampa Tribune, September 2 and 22, 1956; Simon B. Turman, *A Voyage up the Caloosahatchee in 1857*, Tampa Tribune, May 29, 1956; R. E. Rose, *First Dredge in the Everglades*, Everglades News, May 9, 1924; Karl H. Grismer, *The Story of Ft. Myers*, St. Petersburg, 1949; Ft. Myers News-Press January 15 and 30, 1914; Alma Hetherington (daughter of Capt. Paul Gibson), articles by and interviews with; Capt. Edward H. Hall, Jr., correspondence with; Interviews with Capt. Clay Johnson, his daughter Mrs. Roberta J. (Ada) Steffee, Capt. Addison Starr Gilbert, Earl Murray, Cleveland Hicks, Capt. Perry Hull, Homer Guy Hand, Sam Grey, John Chandler, Ralph Blakeley, W. L. Cunningham, A. Q. Howell, Carl T. Cone, Mrs. M. E. Forrey, Mrs. Theresa Edwards, H. O. Ward, Dennis Small, Mr. Jennings (son of Capt. Jennings), George Cason; Henry Ford Museum and Greenfield Village; National Archives; Vessel Information.

POWER BOATS: Arthur L. Fitzhugh, Edwin E. Forbes, Charles Forbes, Ivan L. Van Horn, Carl Lockmiller, Pat Carroll, W. A. Cross, Ray Shackford, Leo Maxwell, Frank O'Connell, T. A. Tillman, F. A. LeFils, Cecil A. Russ, George Graham, Frede Aunapu, L. Francis Herreshoff, Wm. Hunt, *The Real McCoy* by Frederick F. Van de Water, Garden City, N. Y. 1931.

HYACINTHS: *Experience of the Dade County Water Conservation District in Controlling Water Hyacinths*, by F. D. Park, Soil Science Society, Dec. 1954. Miami Herald, April 30, 1950. *Controlling Hyacinthts with 2,4-D in South Florida*, by J. C. Stephens, V. L. Guzman and C. C. Seale, Everglades Experiment Stattion 1955. Capt. Earl Daniels, T. G. Mayo, Bennie A. Williams, Will Addison.

NEW RIVER: U. S. Engineers Chart of New River, 1939. Mrs. Frank Stranahan, Mrs. Bloxam Cromartie, Joe B. Oliver, Frede Aunapu, Ed Hammer, Max Harrelle, Byrd King, Ed. Saar, Wesley W. Stout.

BUS LINES: Mrs. Mary M. Kettner, Srapbook and interviews, Wayne M. Cox, Homer Guy Hand, Everglades News.

ILLUSTRATIONS: Most Steamboat photos are from collections of Capt. Edward H. Hall and Capt. Earl Murray, also from Mrs. Ada Steffee, and Menge Bros. prospectus. Other photos from Ft. Lauderdale Historical Society, John Newhouse collection, etc. Steamer *Suwanee* in Greenfield Village, from Henry Ford Museum, Dearborn, Michigan.

INDEX

INDEX

INDEX

INDEX

INDEX

INDEX

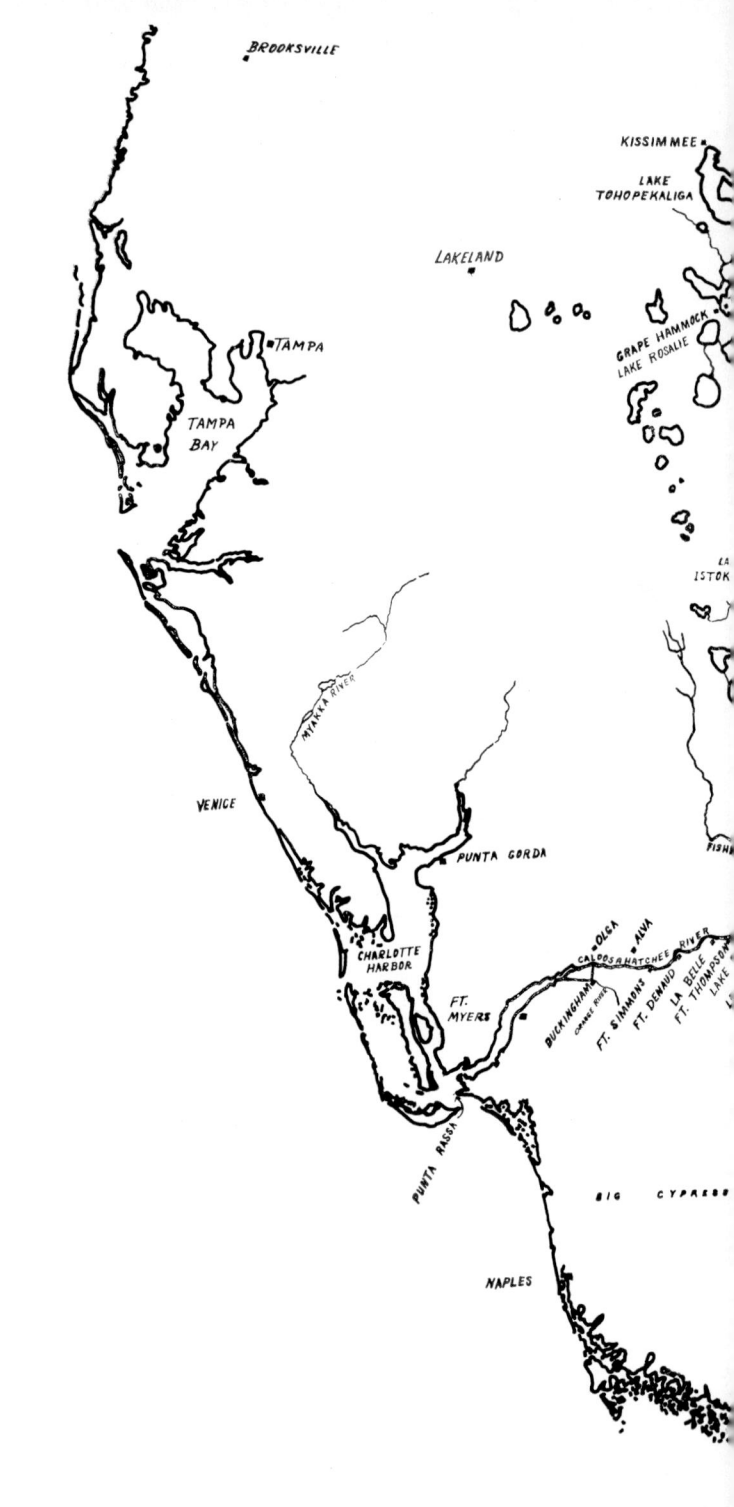